MY NAME

My name is:

_____

- - - - - - - - - - - - - - - - -

_____

These are the letters in my name:

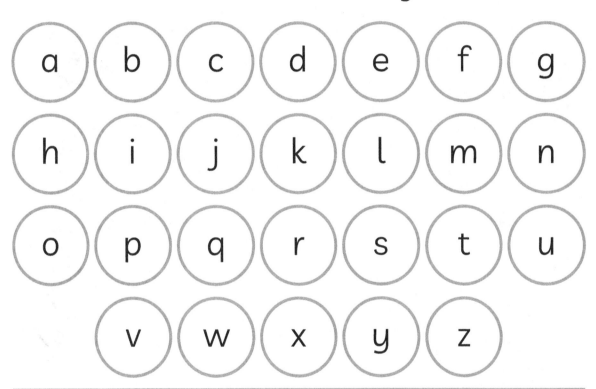

a	b	c	d	e	f	g
h	i	j	k	l	m	n
o	p	q	r	s	t	u
v	w	x	y	z

What does your name mean?

Dab the uppercase A.

Dab the lowercase a.

Trace the letter Aa.

A A A A A

A A A A A

A A A A A

A A A A A

a a a a a

a a a a a

a a a a a

a a a a a

Write the letter Aa.

A A A A A

a a a a a

Dab the uppercase B.

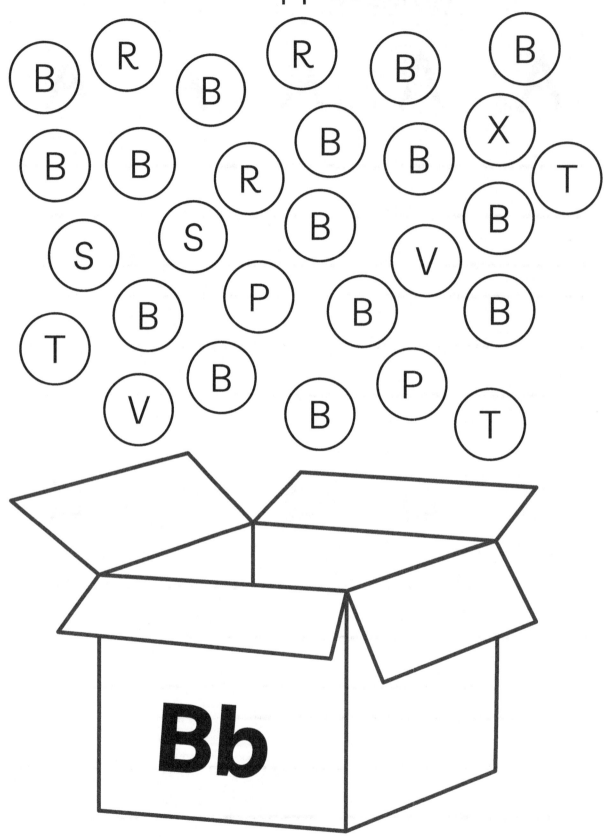

Dab the lowercase b.

Trace the letter Bb.

B B B B B

B B B B B

B B B B B

B B B B B

b b b b b

b b b b b

b b b b b

b b b b b

Write the letter Bb.

B B B B B

b b b b b

Dab the uppercase C.

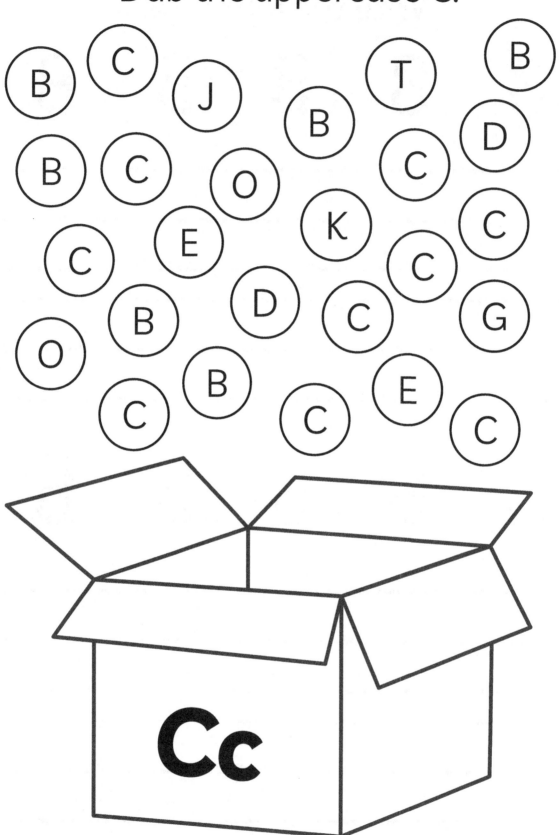

Dab the lowercase c.

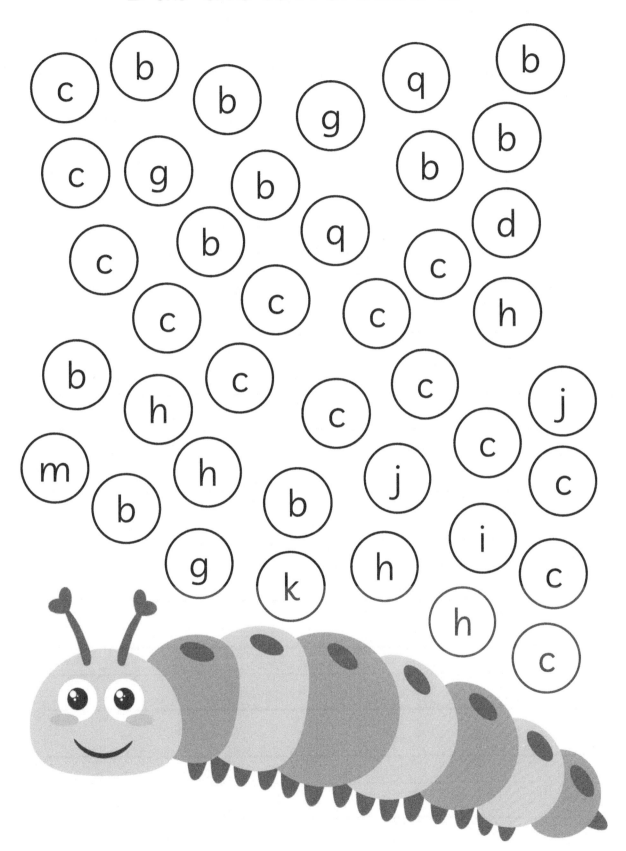

Trace the letter Cc.

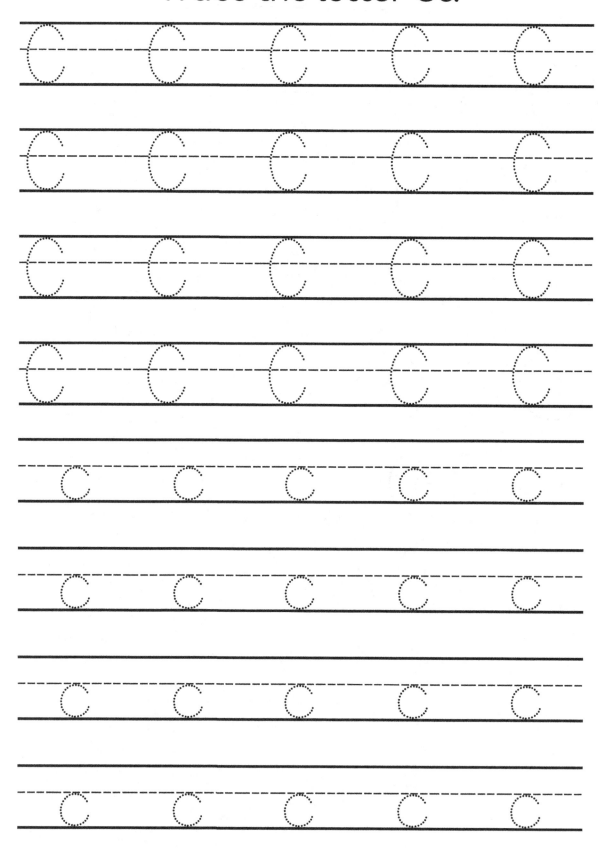

Write the letter Cc.

C C C C C

c c c c c

Dab the uppercase D.

Dab the lowercase d.

d   d   d   d   t   v

t   r   d   t   g   v

g   b   d   r   d

g   b   d   s

b   d   d   d

h   g   d

b   d

s

t

Trace the letter Dd.

Write the letter Dd.

D   D   D   D   D

d   d   d   d   d

Dab the uppercase E.

Dab the lowercase e.

Trace the letter Ee.

Write the letter Ee.

E E E E E

e e e e e

Dab the uppercase F.

Dab the lowercase f.

Trace the letter Ff.

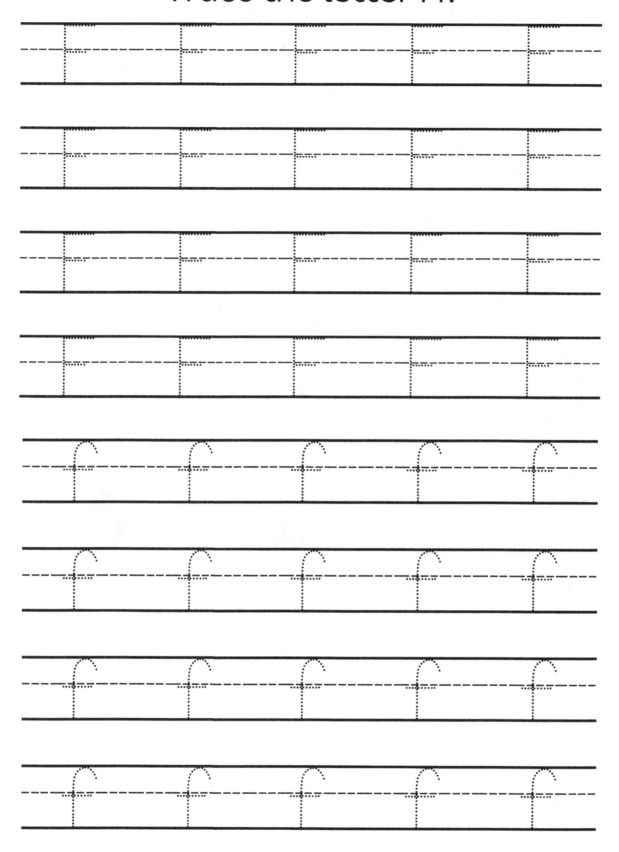

Write the letter Ff.

F F F F F

f f f f f

Dab the uppercase G.

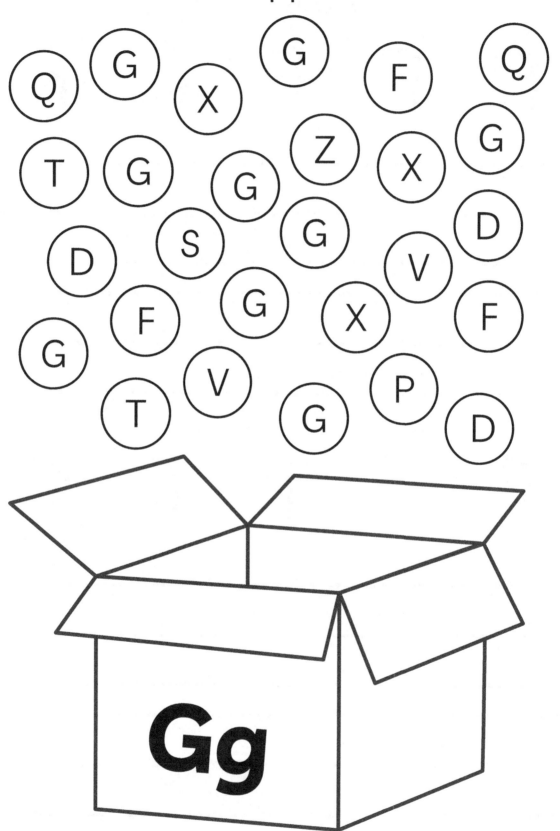

Dab the lowercase g.

Trace the letter Gg.

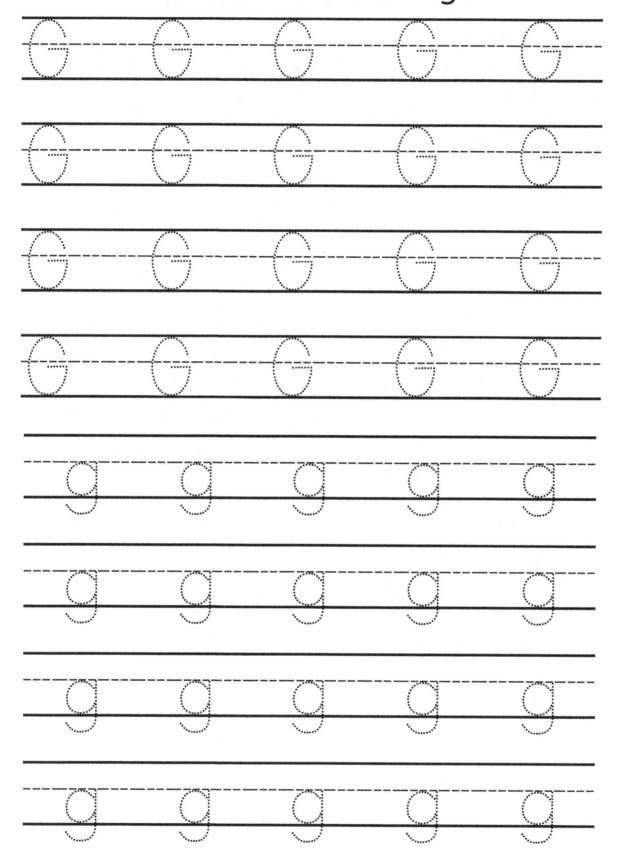

Write the letter Gg.

G G G G G

g g g g g

Dab the uppercase H.

H H X F K M
H T M Z S H
H S M S D
H F H H V H
H K V H K K

Hh

Dab the lowercase h.

Trace the letter Hh.

Write the letter Hh.

H H H H H

h h h h h

Dab the uppercase I.

Dab the lowercase i.

Trace the letter Ii.

Write the letter Ii.

I I I I I

i i i i i

Dab the uppercase J.

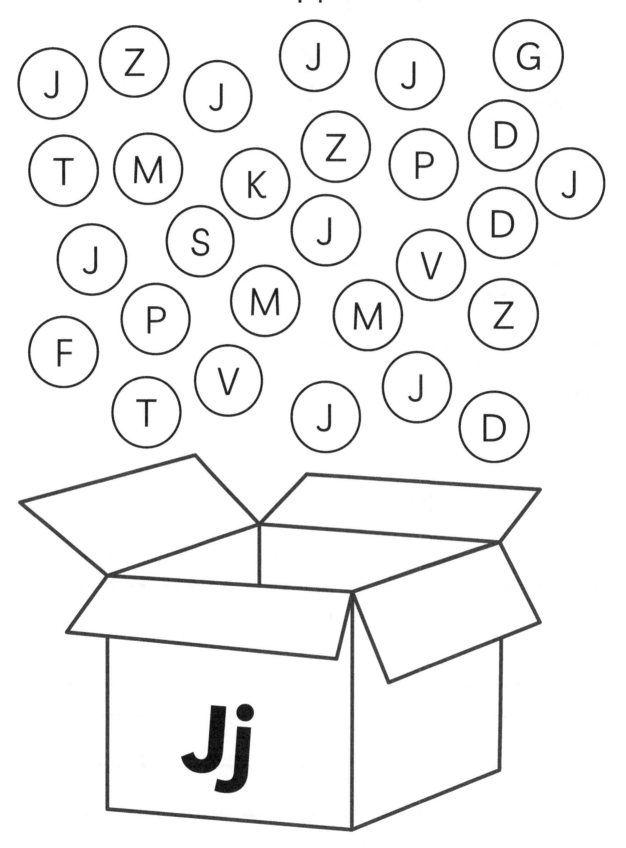

Dab the lowercase j.

Trace the letter Jj.

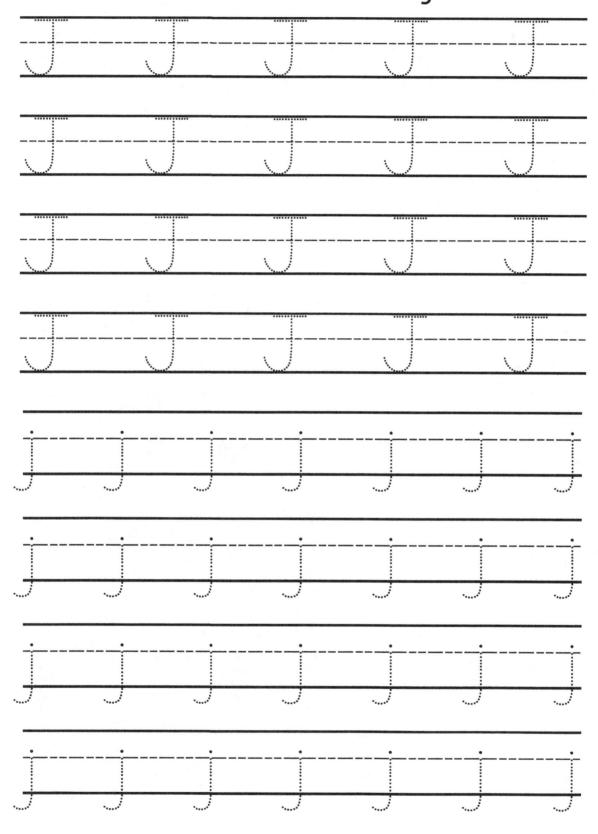

Write the letter Jj.

J J J J J

j j j j j

Dab the uppercase K.

K B X K K P

T B K Z S K

D S K P

P K P F K F

K V B K B

Kk

Dab the lowercase k.

Trace the letter K.

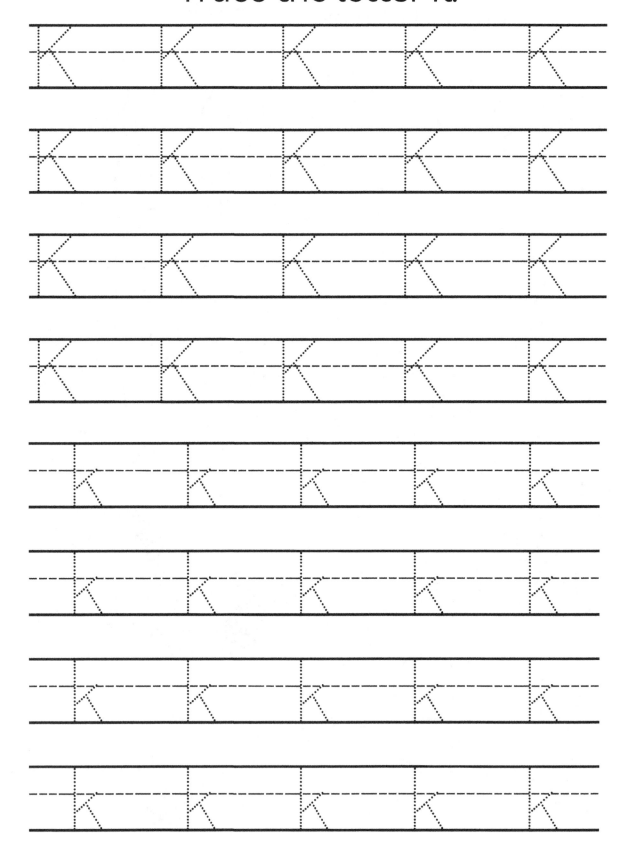

Write the letter Kk.

K K K K K

k k k k k

Dab the uppercase L.

Dab the lowercase l.

Trace the letter Ll.

Write the letter Ll.

L   L   L   L   L

l   l   l   l   l

Dab the uppercase M.

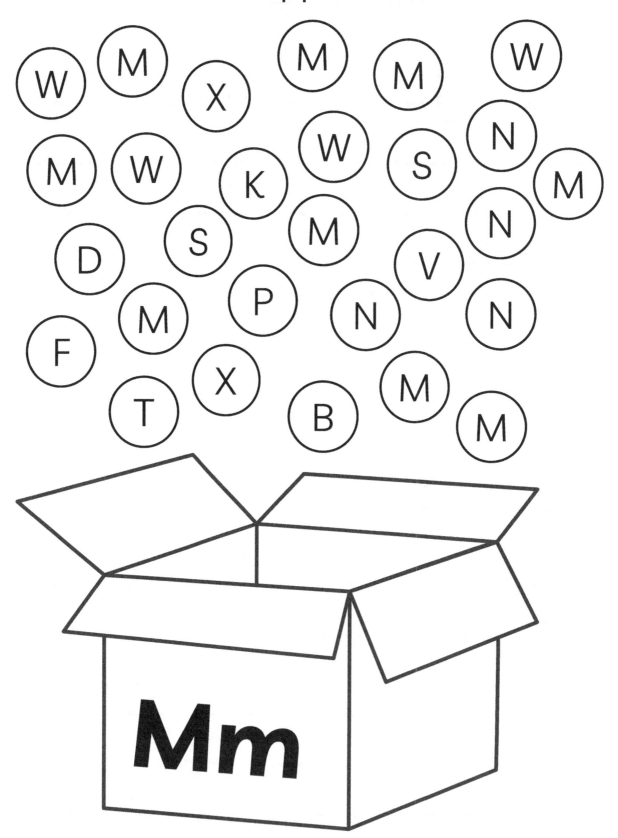

Dab the lowercase m.

Trace the letter Mm.

M — M — M — M — M

M — M — M — M — M

M — M — M — M — M

M — M — M — M — M

m — m — m — m — m

m — m — m — m — m

m — m — m — m — m

m — m — m — m — m

Write the letter Mm.

M M M M M

m m m m m

Dab the uppercase N.

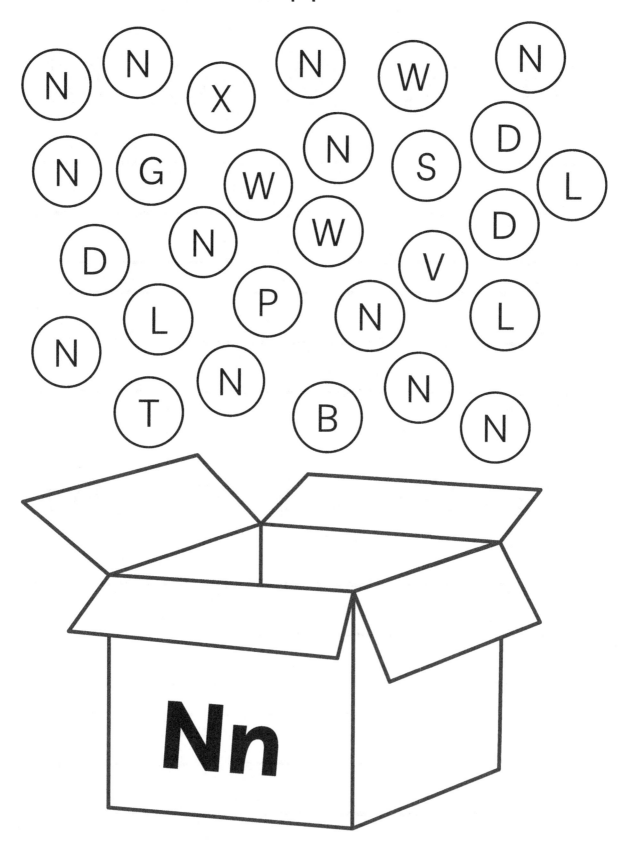

Dab the lowercase n.

Trace the letter Nn.

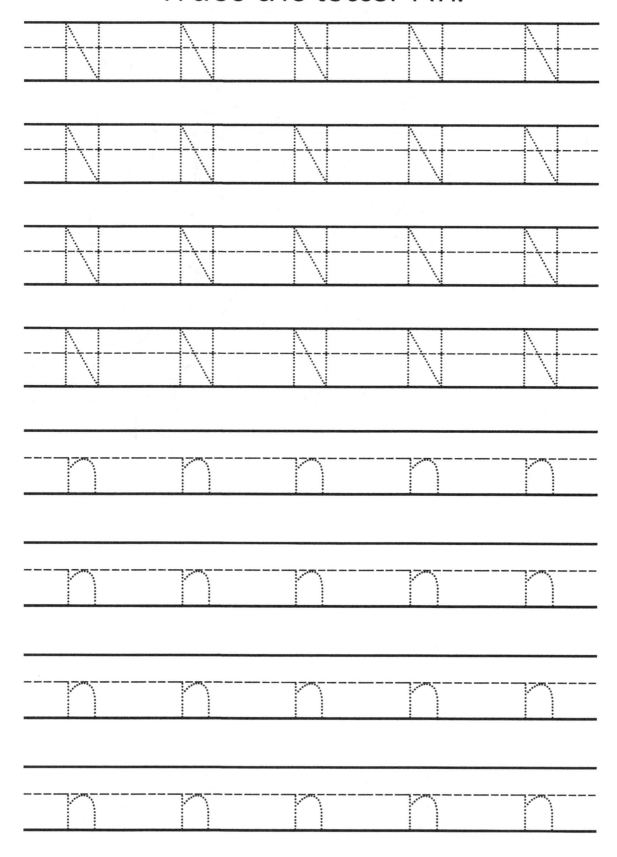

Write the letter Nn.

N   N   N   N   N

n   n   n   n   n

Dab the uppercase O.

Dab the lowercase o.

Trace the letter Oo.

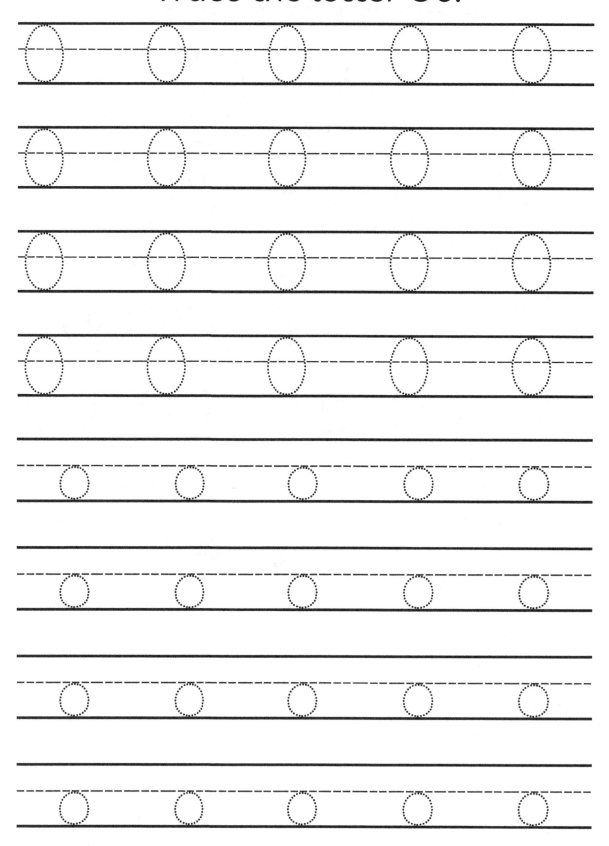

Write the letter Oo.

O   O   O   O   O

o   o   o   o   o

Dab the uppercase P.

Q P X P Q P
P G K Z P D
P S J D
L L P V J
L P Q B P D

Pp

Dab the lowercase p.

p f p p q p
q p t q g p
g j p g f
g s p k
j s
p f
k p
k w
j

Trace the letter Pp.

P P P P P

P P P P P

P P P P P

P P P P P

p p p p p

p p p p p

p p p p p

p p p p p

Write the letter Pp.

P P P P P

p p p p p

Dab the uppercase Q.

Dab the lowercase q.

q q p q q d

q d d q g d

g b d q q f

g g s p q s

b b d d b x q

b g b f

b p

b b w f

q p

w q p

q p q

Trace the letter Qq.

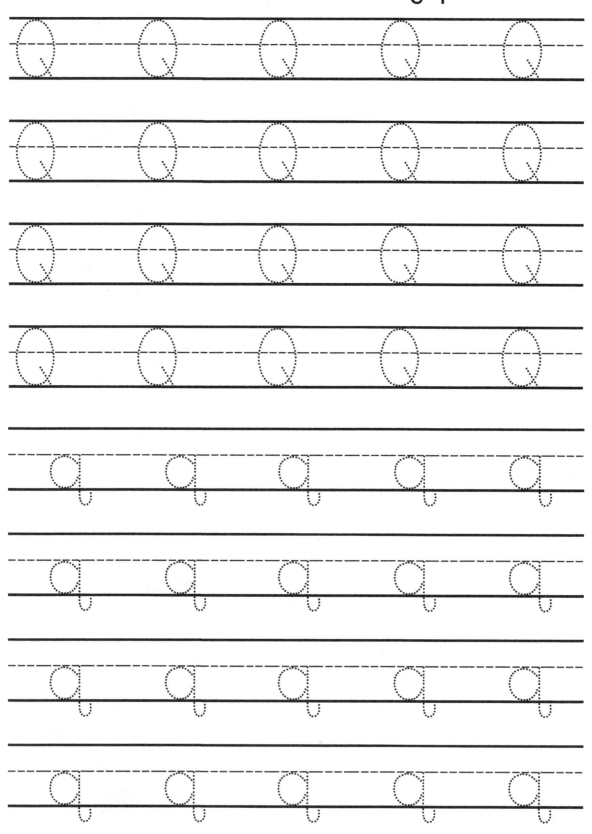

Write the letter Qq.

Q   Q   Q   Q   Q

q   q   q   q   q

Dab the uppercase R.

Dab the lowercase r.

Trace the letter Rr.

R R R R R

R R R R R

R R R R R

R R R R R

r r r r r

r r r r r

r r r r r

r r r r r

Write the letter Rr.

R R R R R

r r r r r

Dab the uppercase S.

L · S · S · S · S · G
S · L · K · T · S · L
D · S · S · S · T
T · P · T · S · S
S · T · S · S · L · D

Ss

Dab the lowercase s.

s   s   s   s   q   f
k   r   y   s   k   s
    x   b   k   f
    y   s   s   p   s
b   s   s   x   f
s   x   x
p
k   s
    s
w   p
k   p

Trace the letter Ss.

S S S S S

S S S S S

S S S S S

S S S S S

S S S S S

S S S S S

S S S S S

S S S S S

Write the letter Ss.

S S S S S

S S S S S

Dab the uppercase T.

K P X R K K

T R T X T D

P S J V K

T T P P T J

T T R T X R

Tt

Dab the lowercase t.

Trace the letter Tt.

Write the letter Tt.

T T T T T

t t t t t

Dab the uppercase U.

U I I E I E
A A A U O E
E U A E O U
U O U U
A O U O U

Uu

Dab the lowercase u.

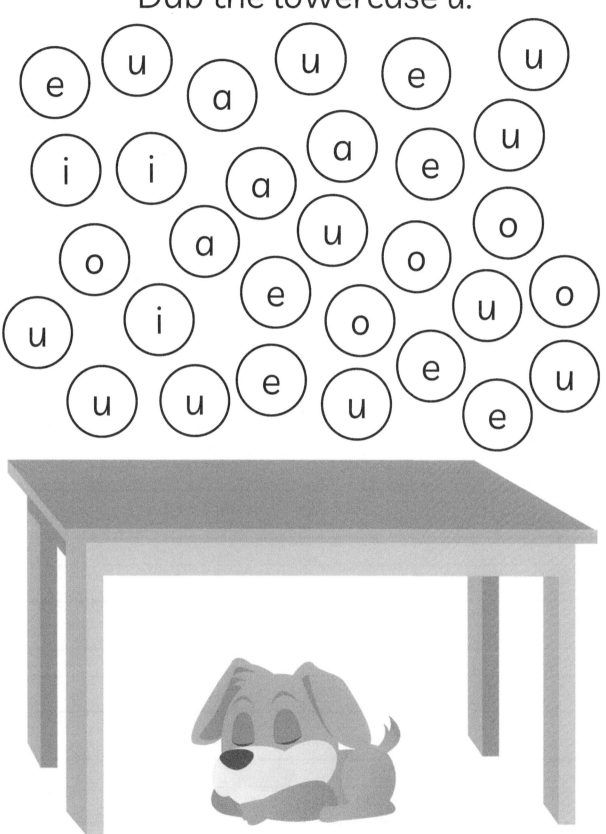

Trace the letter Uu.

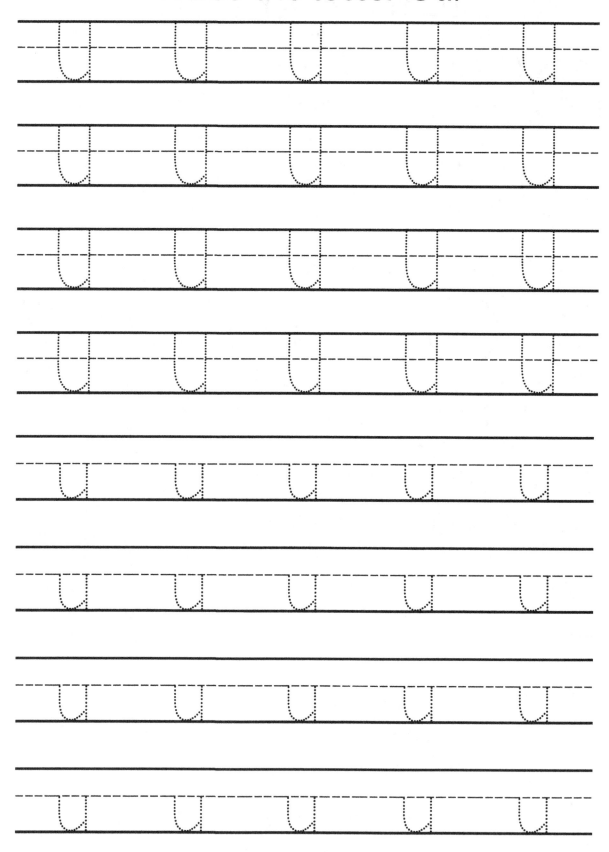

Write the letter Uu.

u u u u u

u u u u u

Dab the uppercase V.

B V Y S V Y

V G S V P V

P B J V D

P V P S V

V Q V P V

Vv

Dab the lowercase v.

Trace the letter Vv.

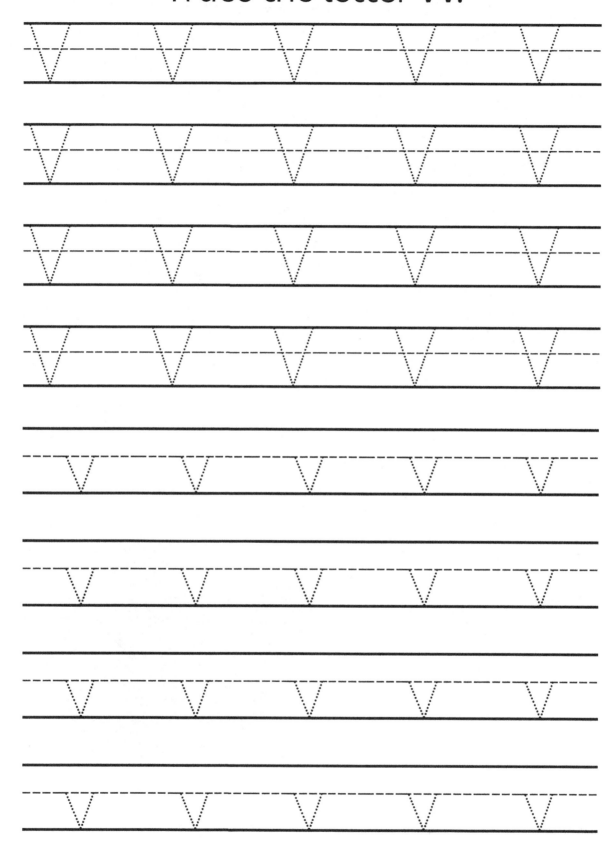

Write the letter Vv.

V V V V V

V V V V V

Dab the uppercase W.

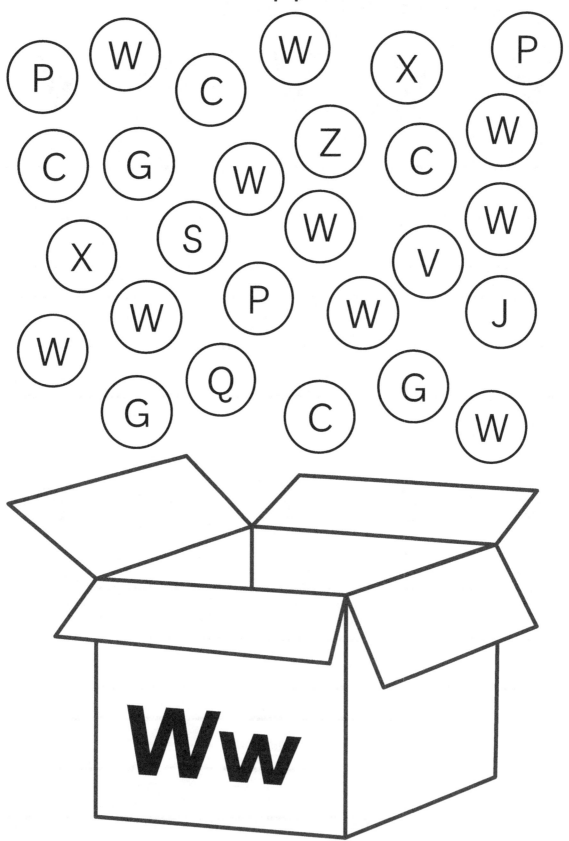

Dab the lowercase w.

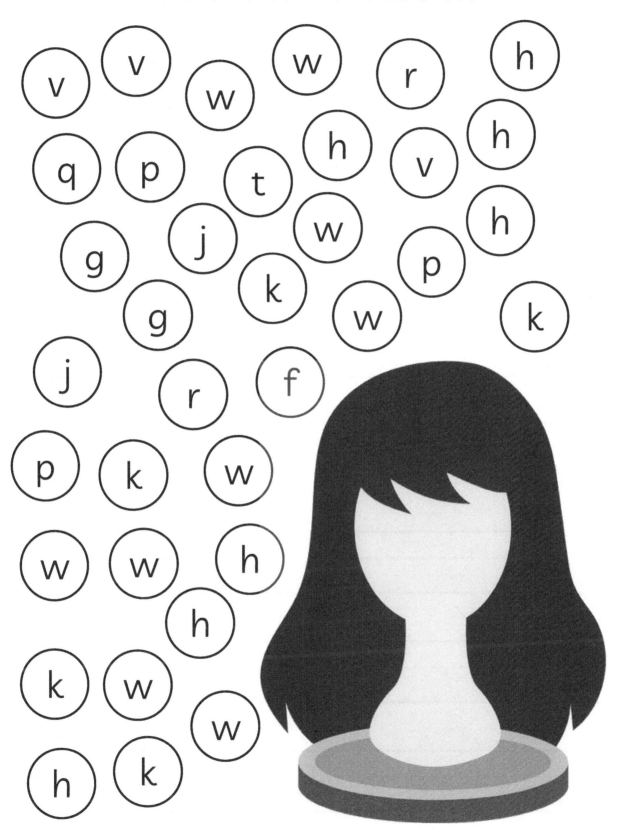

Trace the letter Ww.

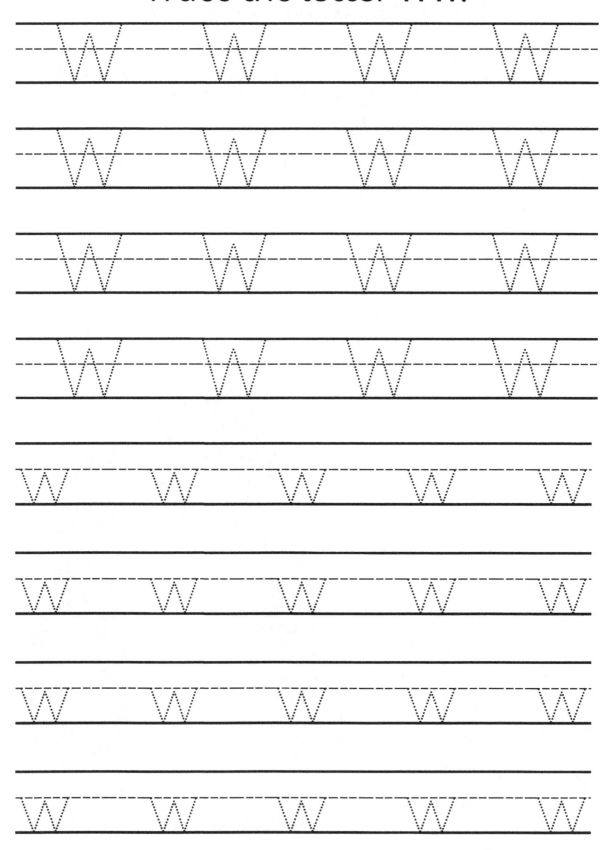

Write the letter Ww.

W W W W W

w w w w w

Dab the uppercase X.

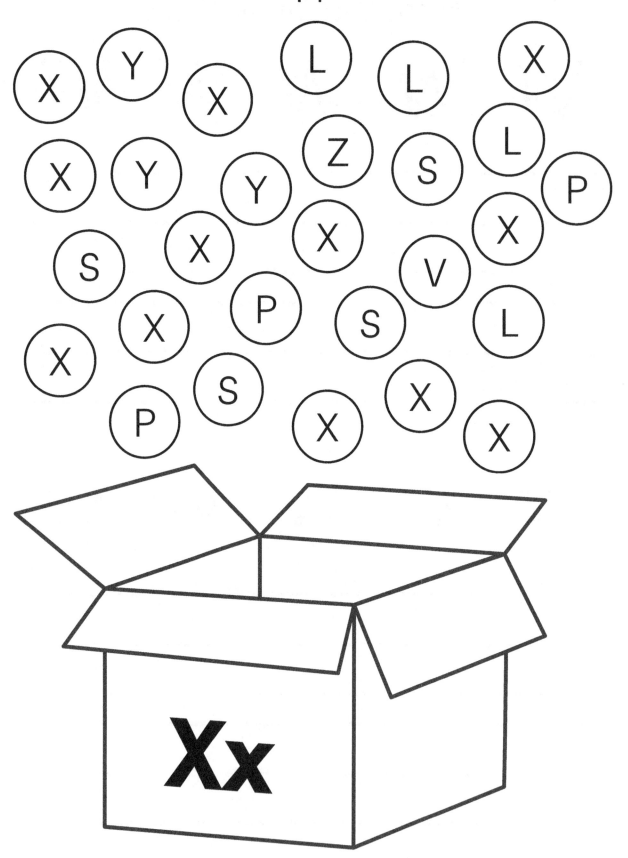

Dab the lowercase x.

Trace the letter Xx.

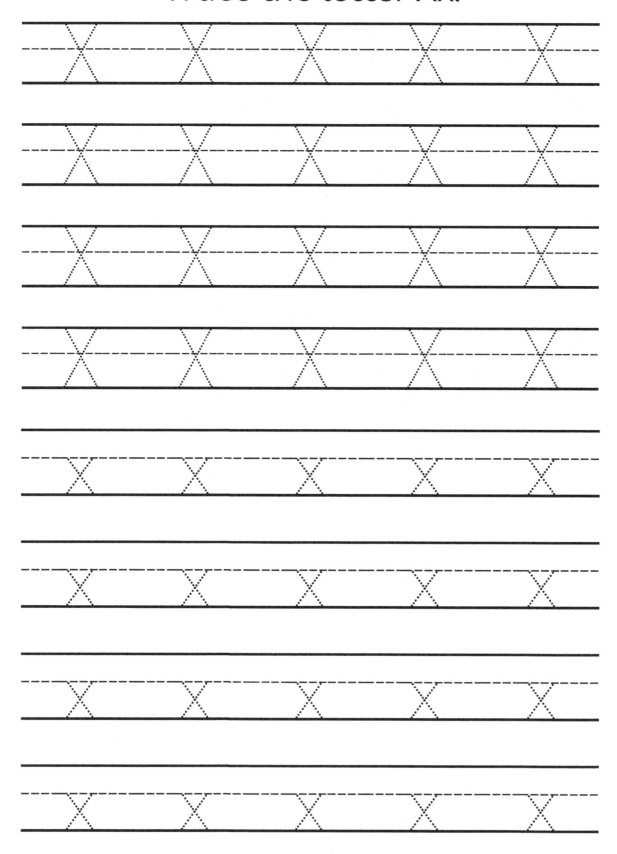

Write the letter Xx.

X   X   X   X   X

x   x   x   x   x

Trace the letter Yy.

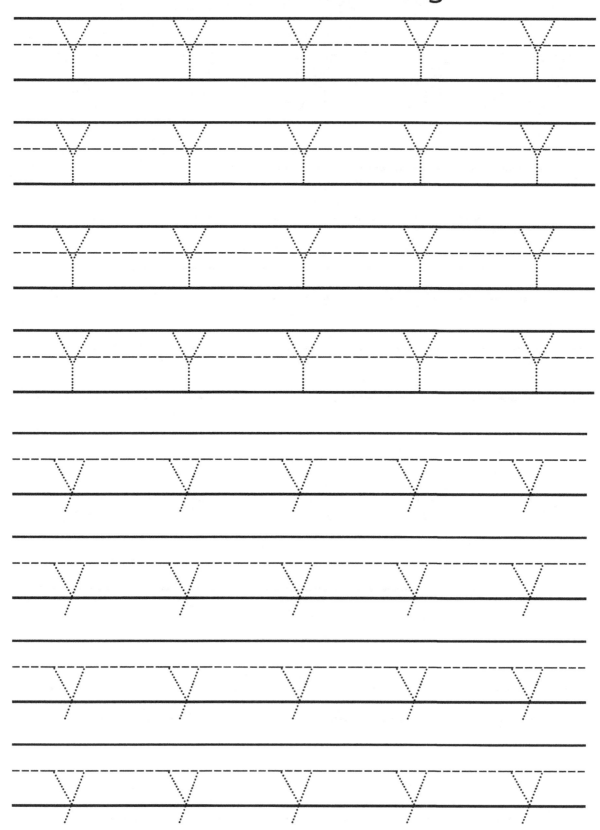

Dab the uppercase Y.

Dab the lowercase y.

Write the letter Yy.

Y   Y   Y   Y   Y

y   y   y   y   y

Dab the uppercase Z.

N N X Z Z Z
Z K Z Z Z N
N S Z N V K
L L P Z K
Z H H Z Z

Zz

Dab the lowercase z.

Trace the letter Zz.

Write the letter Zz.

Z Z Z Z Z

z z z z z

ALPHABET ORDER

Trace the letters of the alphabet.

A	B	C	D	E	F
G	H	I	J	K	L
M	N	O	P	Q	R
S	T	U	V	W	X
Y	Z				

ALPHABET ORDER

Trace the letters of the alphabet.

a	b	c	d	e	f
g	h	i	j	k	l
m	n	o	p	q	r
s	t	u	v	w	x
y	z				

TRACING NUMBERS

Count the item and trace the number word.

I

one

Trace the number.

TRACING NUMBERS

Count the items and trace the number word.

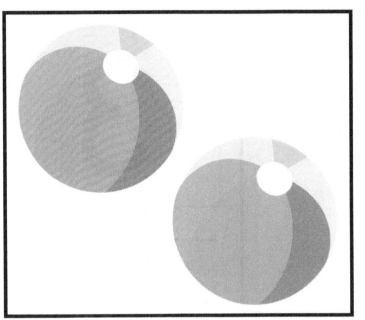

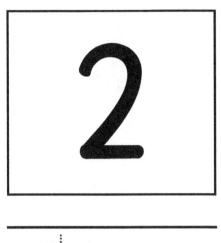

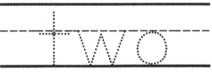

Trace the number.

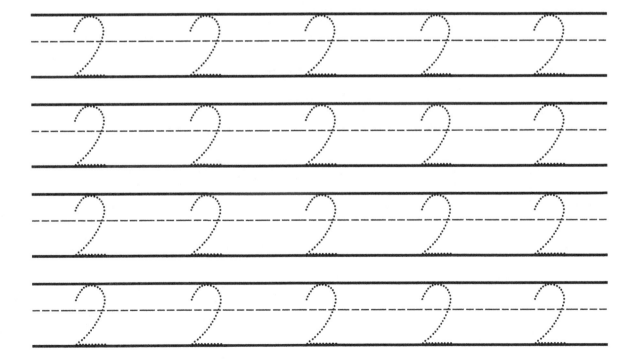

TRACING NUMBERS

Count the items and trace the number word.

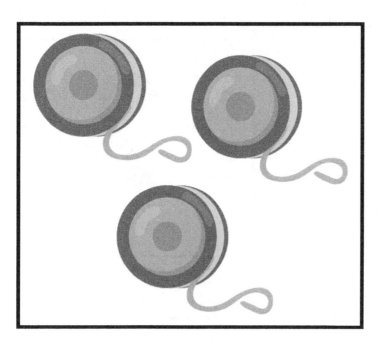

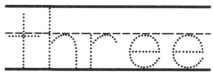

Trace the number.

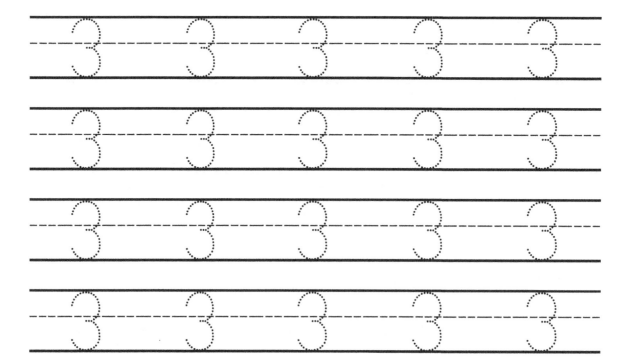

TRACING NUMBERS

Count the items and trace the number word.

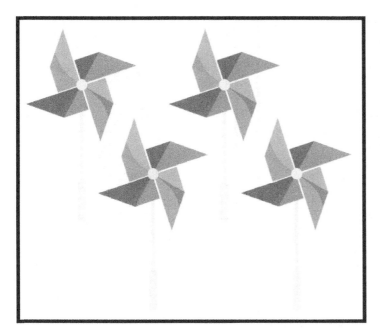

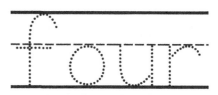

Trace the number.

TRACING NUMBERS

Count the items and trace the number word.

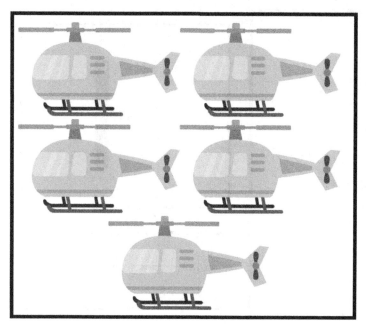

five

Trace the number.

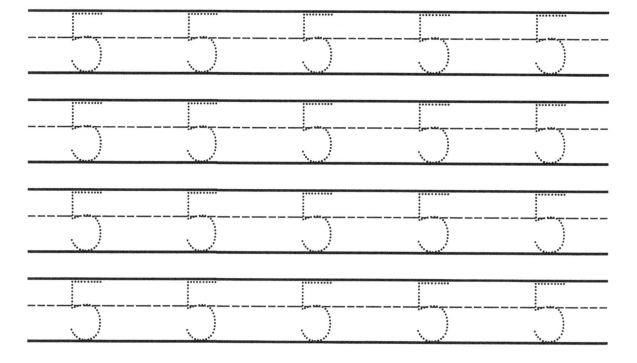

TRACING NUMBERS

Count the items and trace the number word.

six

Trace the number.

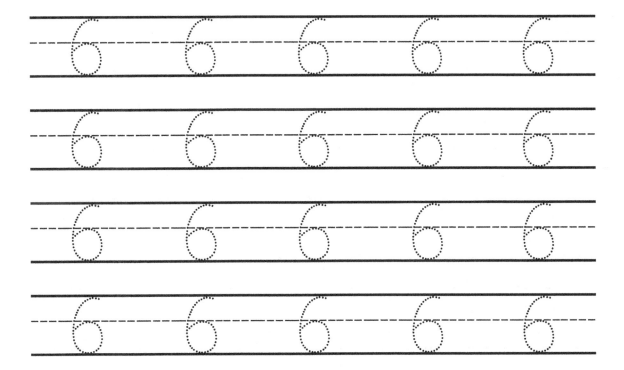

TRACING NUMBERS

Count the items and trace the number word.

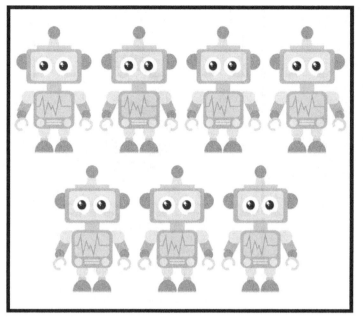

seven

Trace the number.

7 7 7 7 7

7 7 7 7 7

7 7 7 7 7

7 7 7 7 7

TRACING NUMBERS

Count the items and trace the number word.

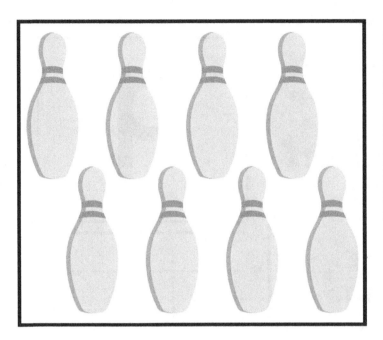

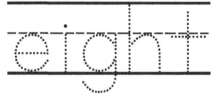

Trace the number.

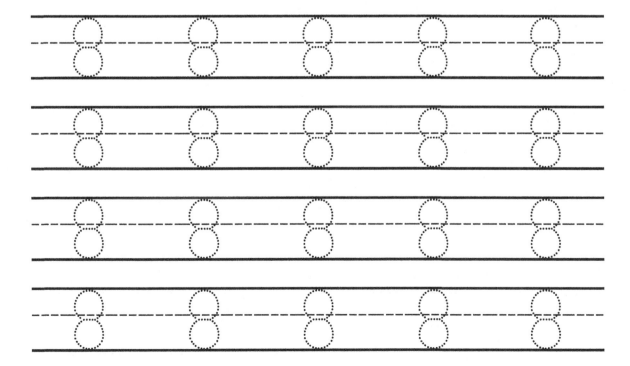

TRACING NUMBERS

Count the items and trace the number word.

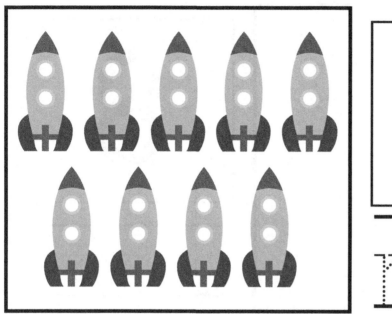

Trace the number.

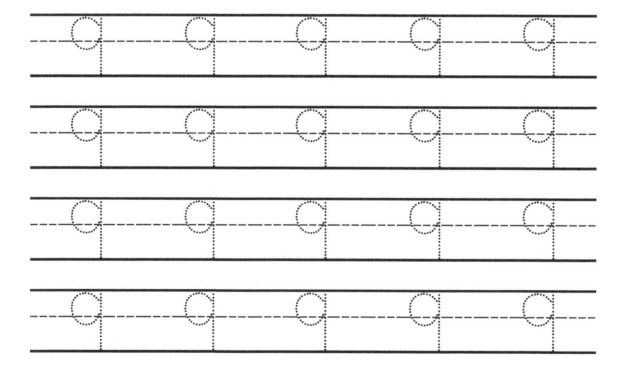

TRACING NUMBERS

Count the items and trace the number word.

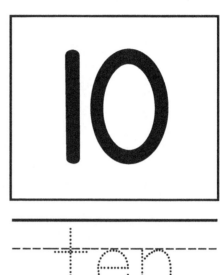

ten

Trace the number.

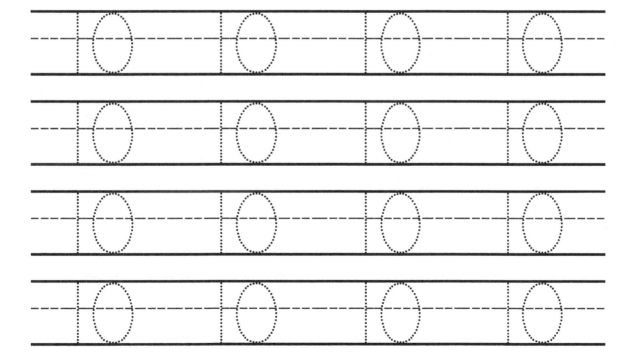

TRACING NUMBERS

Count the items and trace the number word.

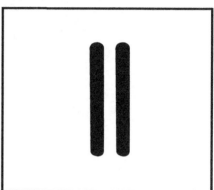

eleven

Trace the number.

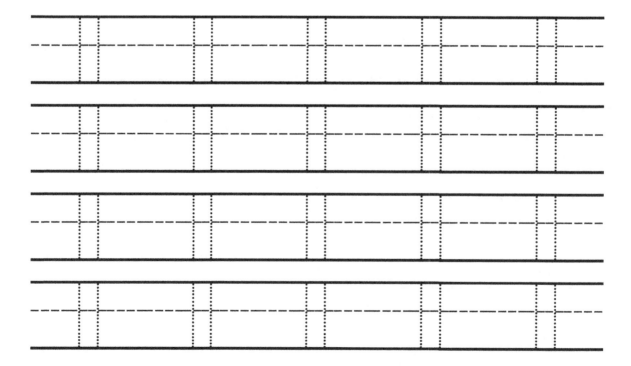

TRACING NUMBERS

Count the items and trace the number word.

twelve

Trace the number.

TRACING NUMBERS

Count the items and trace the number word.

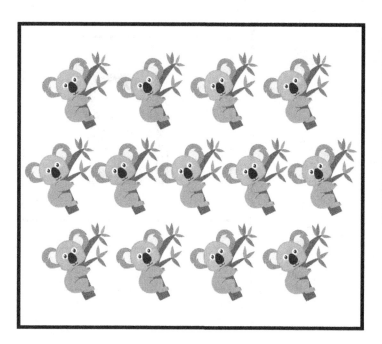

Thirteen

Trace the number.

3   3   3   3

3   3   3   3

3   3   3   3

3   3   3   3

TRACING NUMBERS

Count the items and trace the number word.

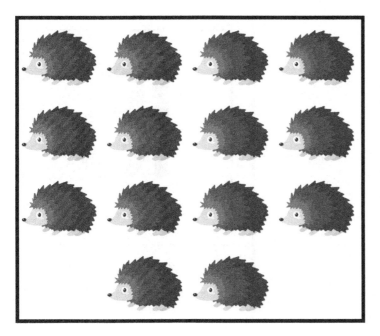

fourteen

Trace the number.

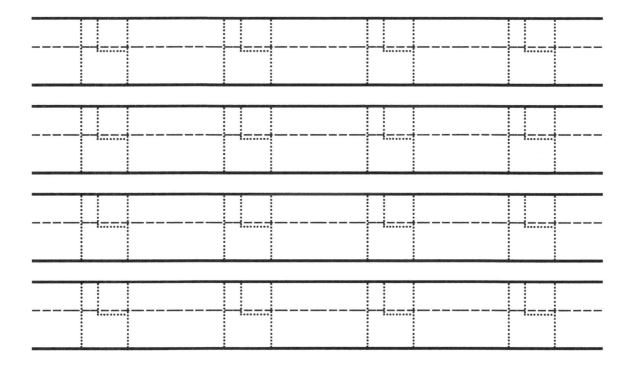

TRACING NUMBERS

Count the items and trace the number word.

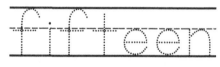

Trace the number.

TRACING NUMBERS

Count the items and trace the number word.

sixteen

Trace the number.

16 16 16 16

16 16 16 16

16 16 16 16

16 16 16 16

TRACING NUMBERS

Count the items and trace the number word.

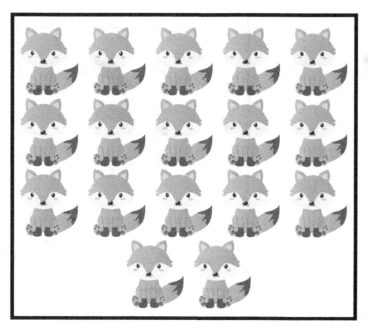

seventeen

Trace the number.

7 7 7 7

7 7 7 7

7 7 7 7

7 7 7 7

TRACING NUMBERS

Count the items and trace the number word.

eighteen

Trace the number.

TRACING NUMBERS

Count the items and trace the number word.

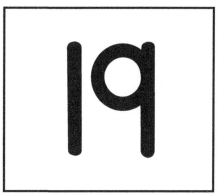

nineteen

Trace the number.

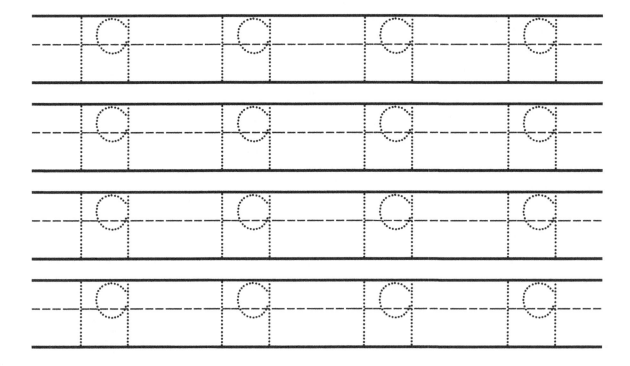

TRACING NUMBERS

Count the items and trace the number word.

Trace the number.

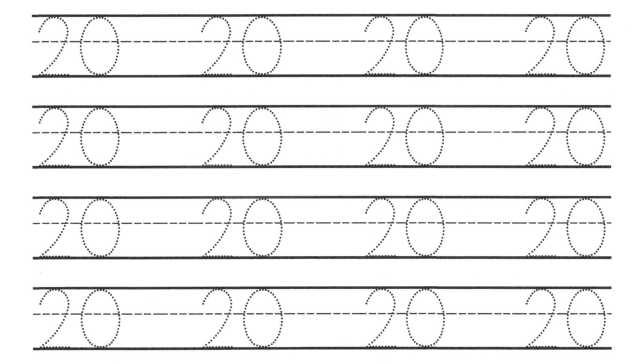

WRITING NUMBERS

Write the numbers 1 to 10.

1	2	3	4	5
6	7	8	9	10

WRITING NUMBERS

Write the numbers 11 to 20.

11	12	13	14	15
16	17	18	19	20

WRITING NUMBER WORDS

Trace and write the number names 1 to 10.

1	one	**one**
2	two	
3	three	
4	four	
5	five	
6	six	
7	seven	
8	eight	
9	nine	
10	ten	

WRITING NUMBER WORDS

Trace and write the number names 11 to 20.

11	eleven	**eleven**
12	twelve	
13	thirteen	
14	fourteen	
15	fifteen	
16	sixteen	
17	seventeen	
18	eighteen	
19	nineteen	
20	twenty	

NUMBER ORDER

Fill in the missing number in the sequence.

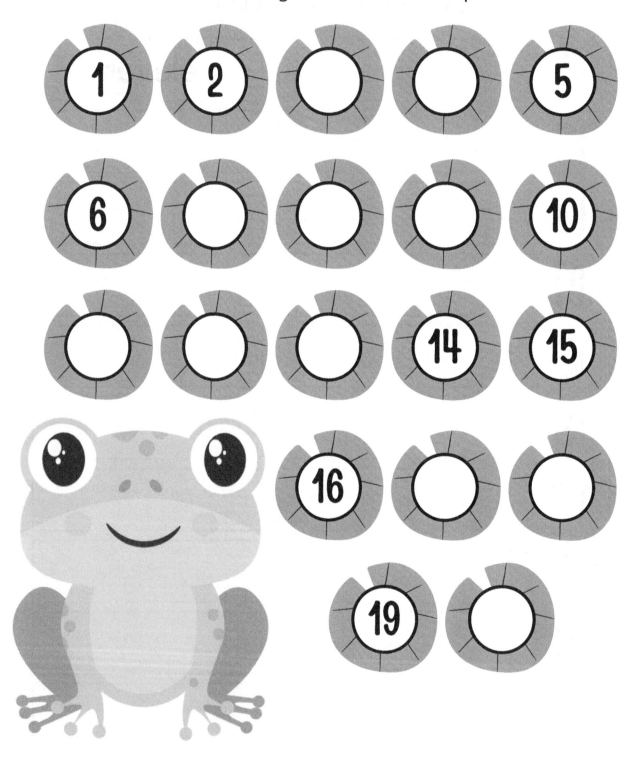

NUMBER ORDER

Fill in the missing number in the sequence.

NUMBER ORDER

Fill in the missing number in the sequence.

ORDERING NUMBERS

Cut and glue in order.

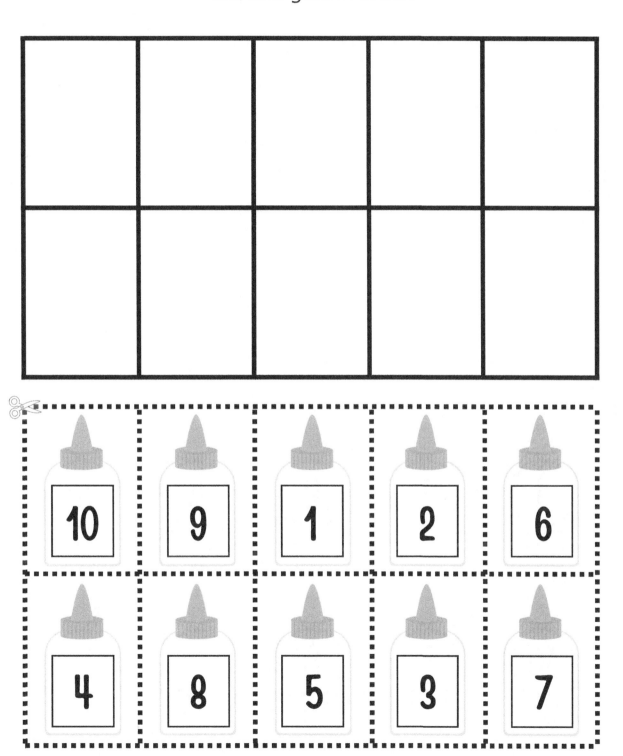

ORDERING NUMBERS

Cut and glue in order.

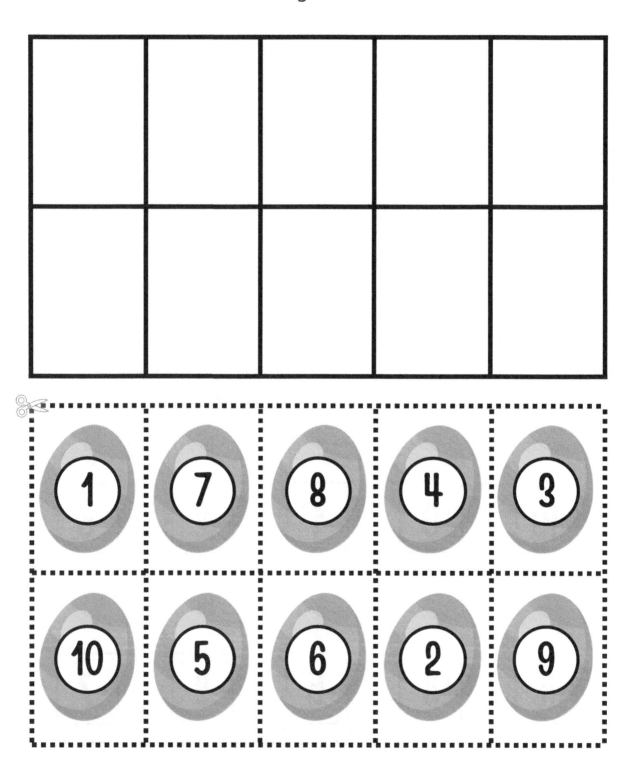

ORDERING NUMBERS

Cut and glue in order.

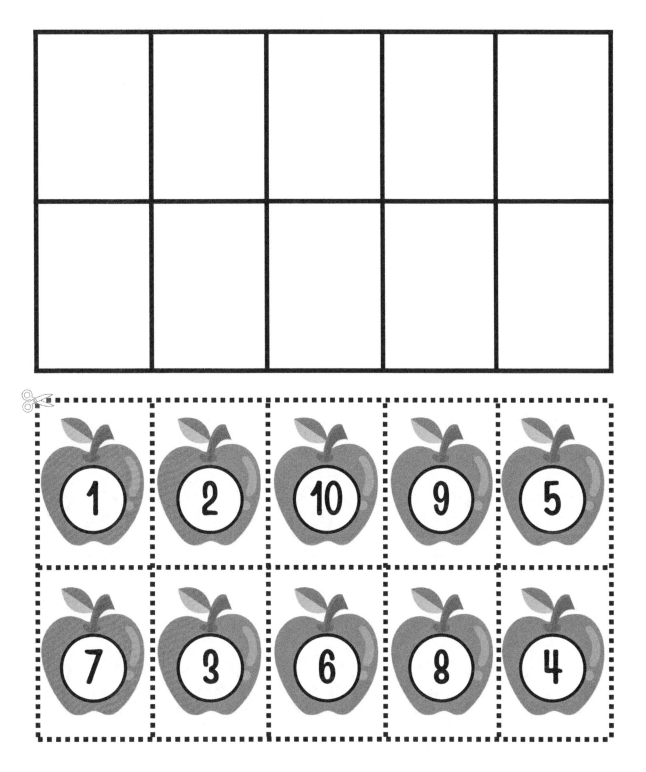

ORDERING NUMBERS

Cut and glue in order.

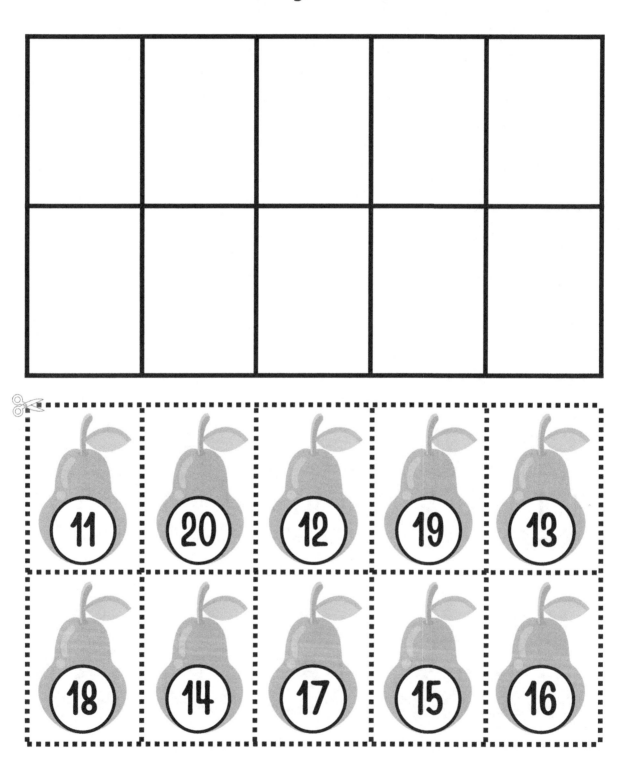

ORDERING NUMBERS

Cut and glue in order.

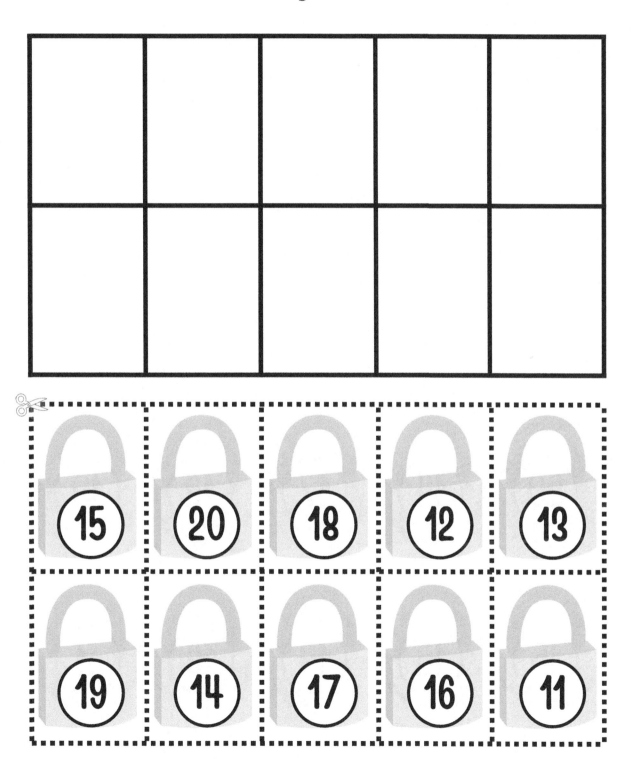

ORDERING NUMBERS

Cut and glue in order.

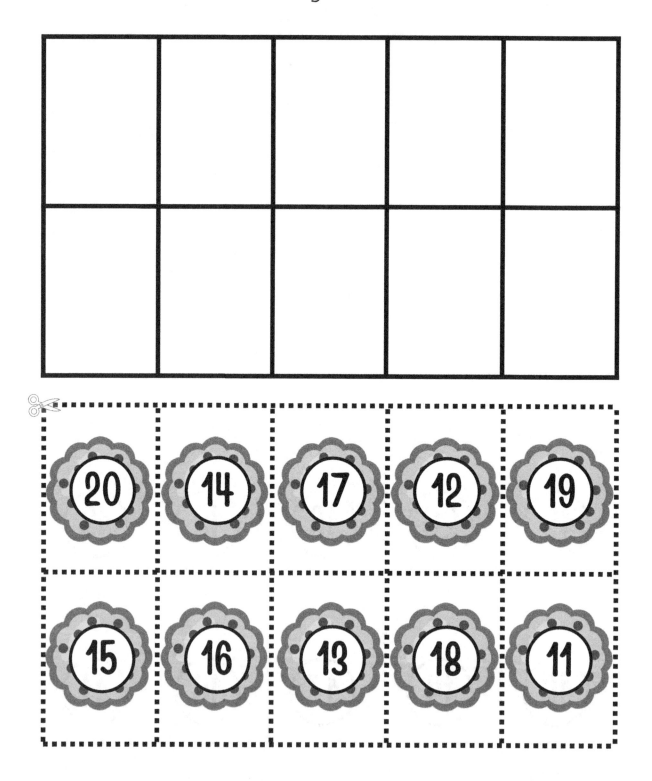

NUMBER BEFORE

Fill in the number that comes before.

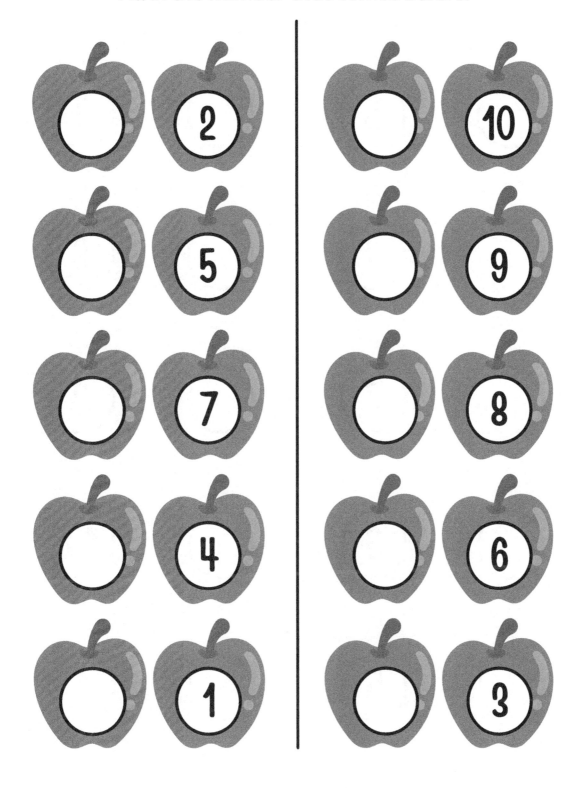

NUMBER BEFORE

Fill in the number that comes before.

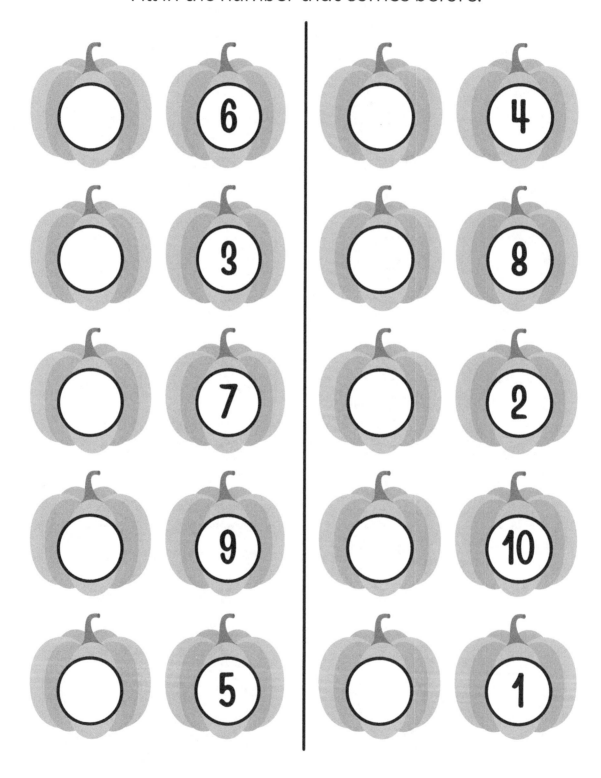

NUMBER BEFORE

Fill in the number that comes before.

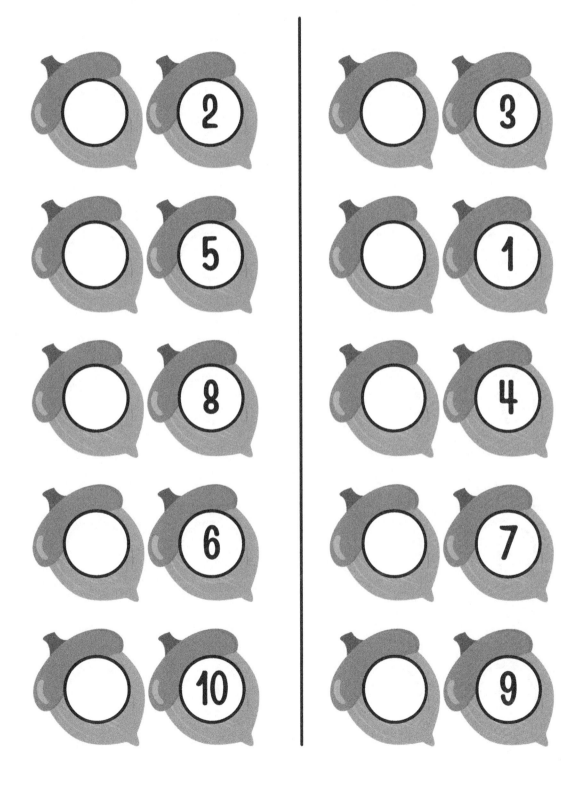

NUMBER AFTER

Fill in the number that comes after.

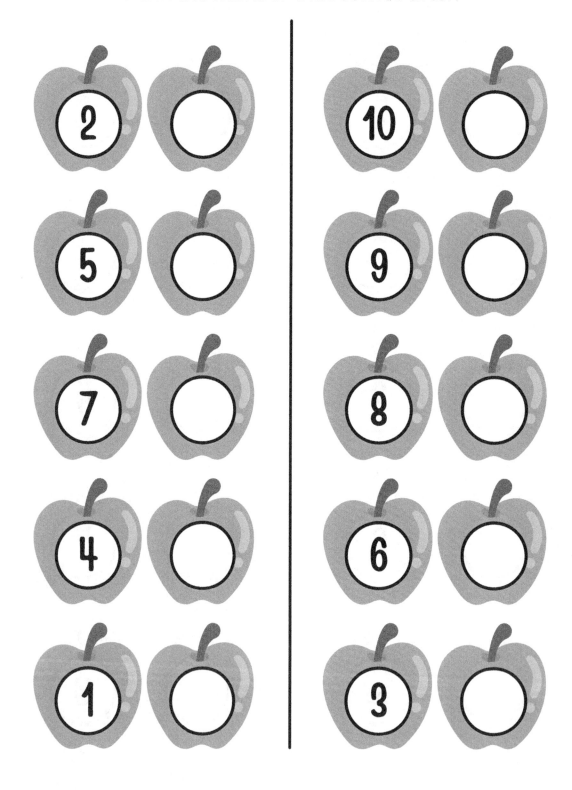

NUMBER AFTER

Fill in the number that comes after.

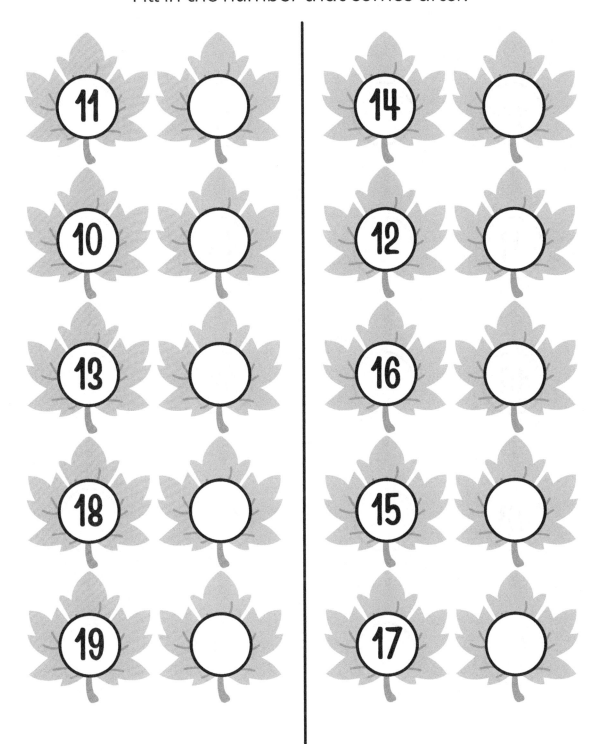

NUMBER AFTER

Fill in the number that comes after.

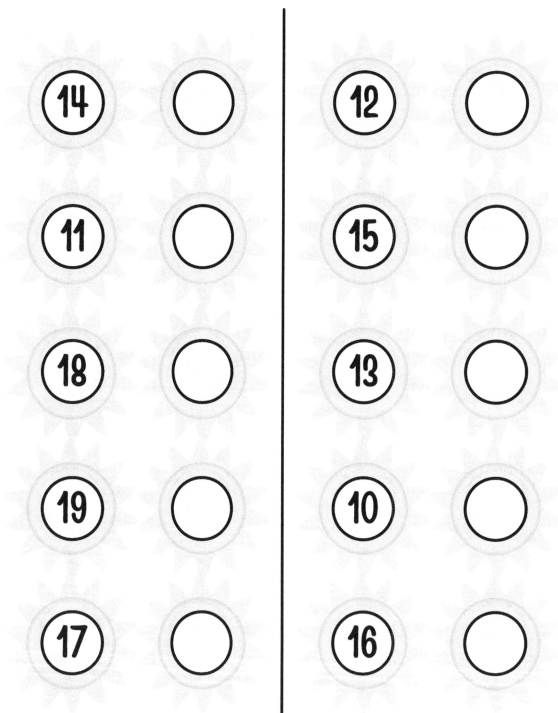

NUMBER BETWEEN

Fill in the number that comes between.

2		4

7		9

3		5

6		8

NUMBER BETWEEN

Fill in the number that comes between.

1		3

5		7

0		2

4		6

NUMBER BETWEEN

Fill in the number that comes between.

8		10

9		11

13		15

10		12

NUMBER BETWEEN

Fill in the number that comes between.

11		13

15		17

12		14

14		16

ADDITION TO 5

Count the pictures. Add and write the correct sum in the box.

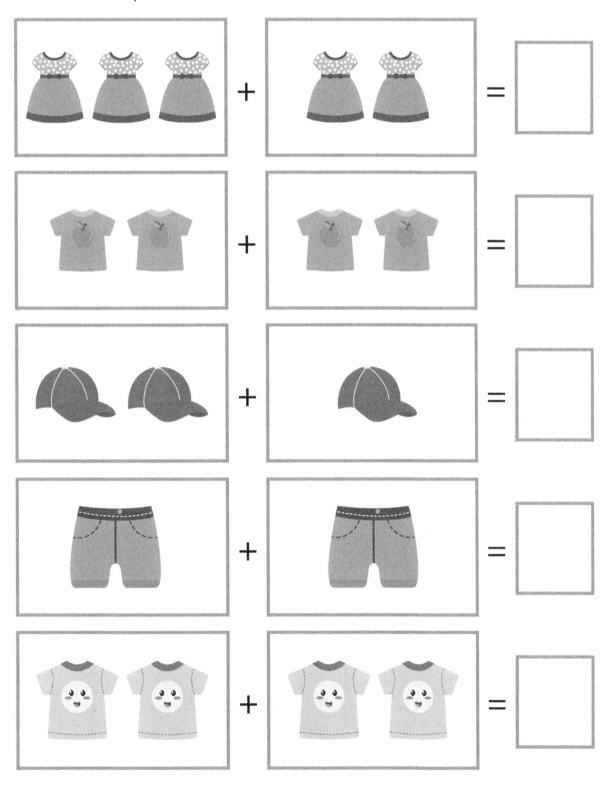

ADDITION TO 5

Count the pictures. Add and write the correct sum in the box.

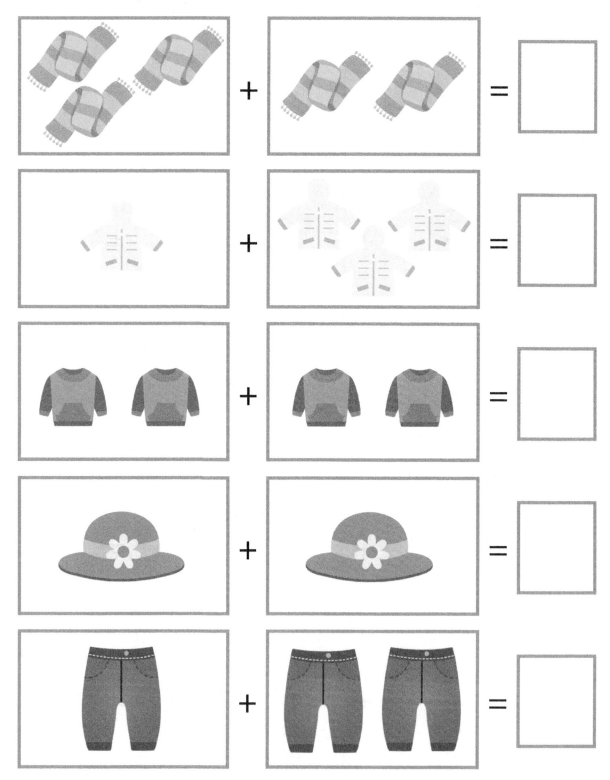

ADDITION TO 5

Count the pictures. Add and write the correct sum in the box.

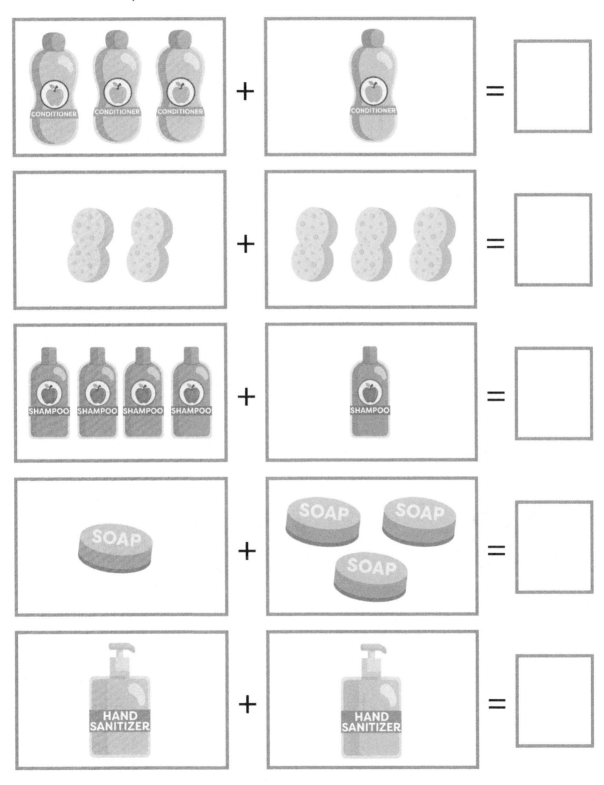

ADDITION TO 5

Count the pictures. Add and write the correct sum in the box.

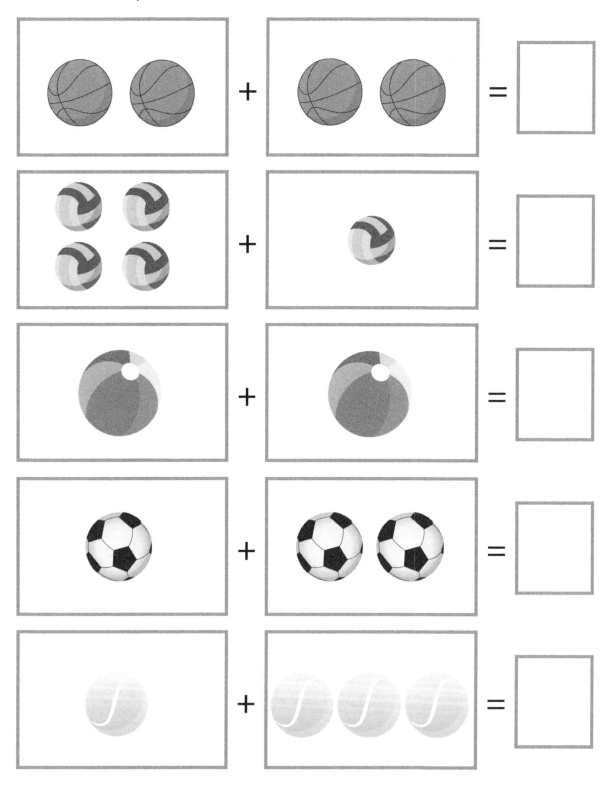

ADDITION TO 5

Count the pictures. Add and write the correct sum in the box.

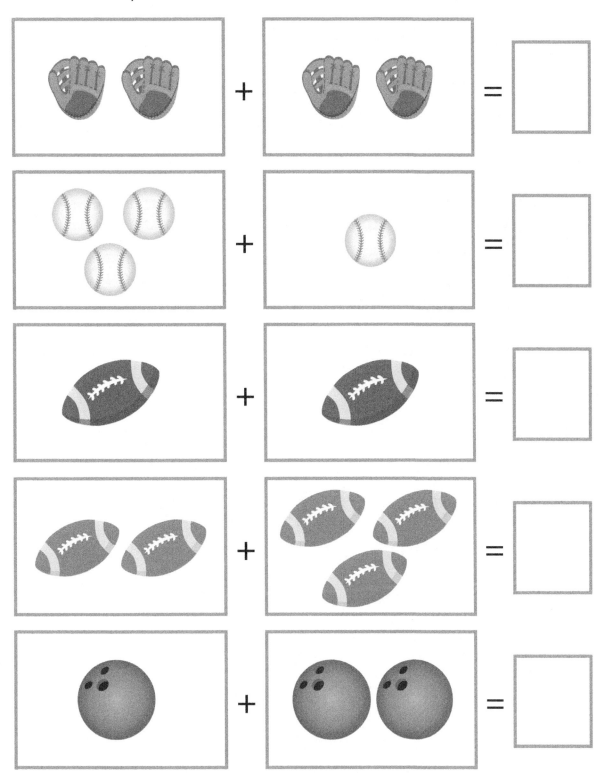

ADDITION TO 10

Count the pictures. Add and write the correct sum in the box.

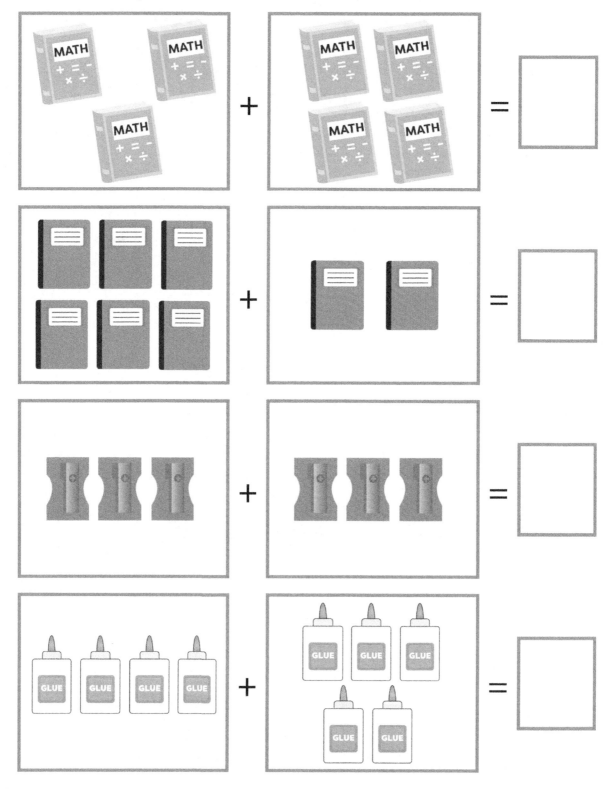

ADDITION TO 10

Count the pictures. Add and write the correct sum in the box.

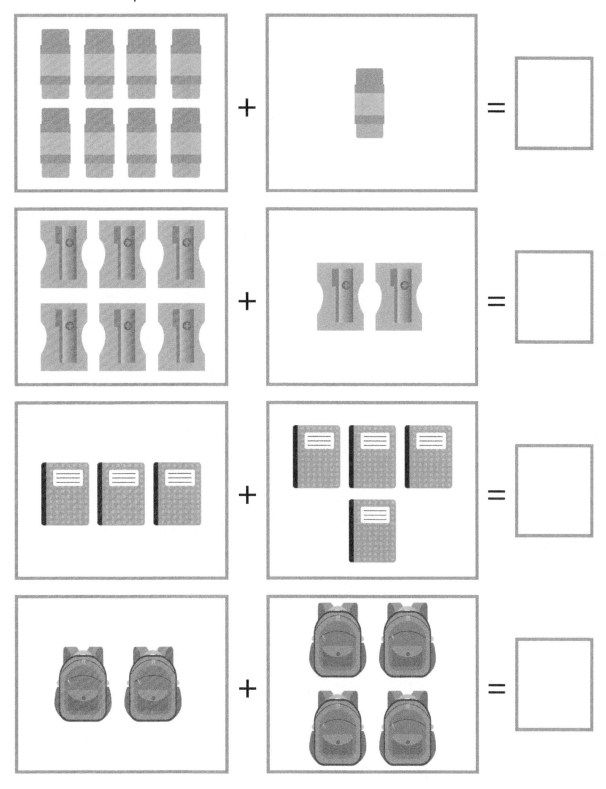

ADDITION TO 10

Count the pictures. Add and write the correct sum in the box.

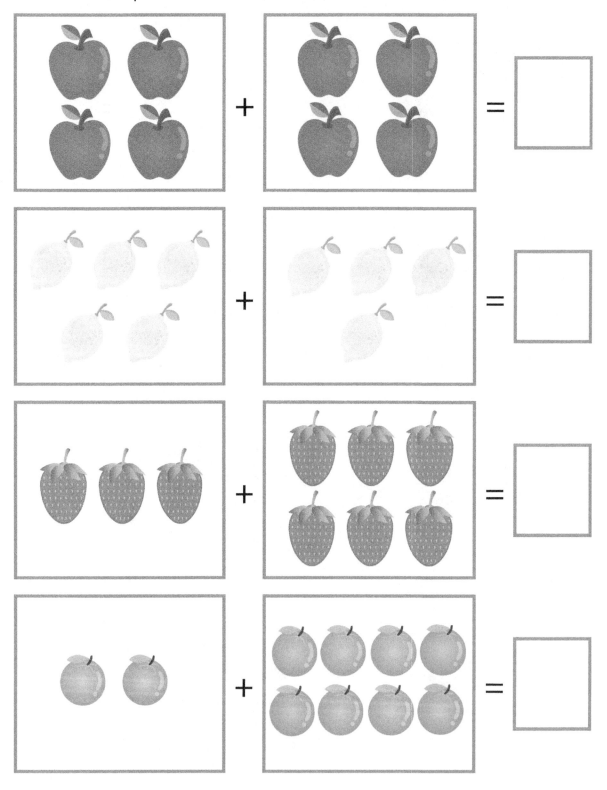

ADDITION TO 10

Count the pictures. Add and write the correct sum in the box.

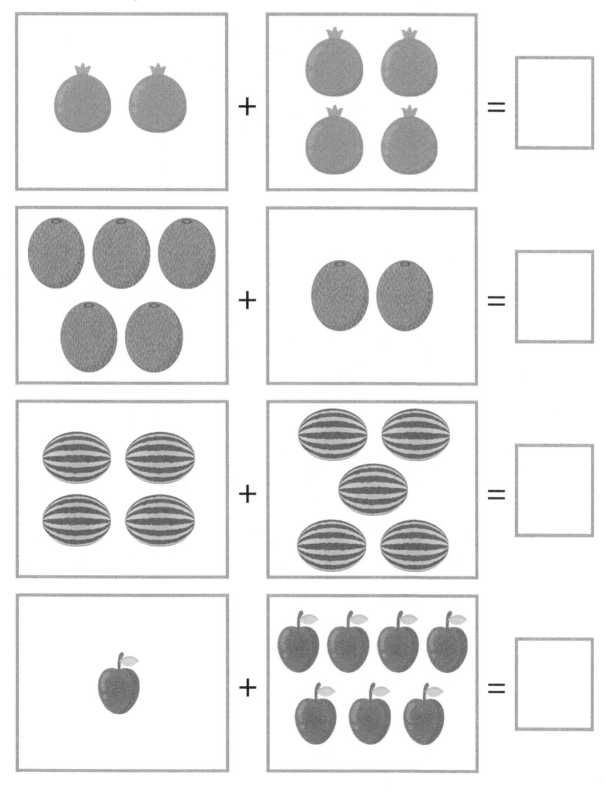

ADDITION TO 10

Count the pictures. Add and write the correct sum in the box.

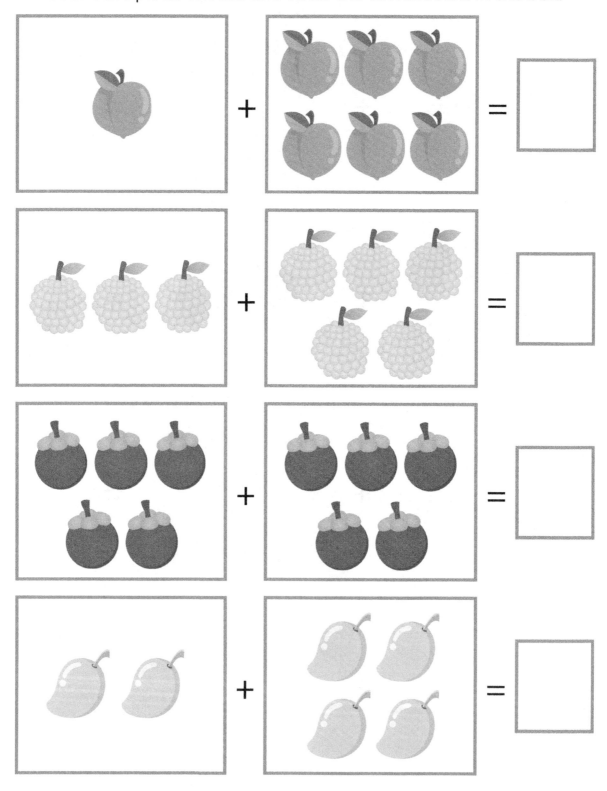

ADDITION TO 15

Count the pictures. Add and write the correct sum in the box.

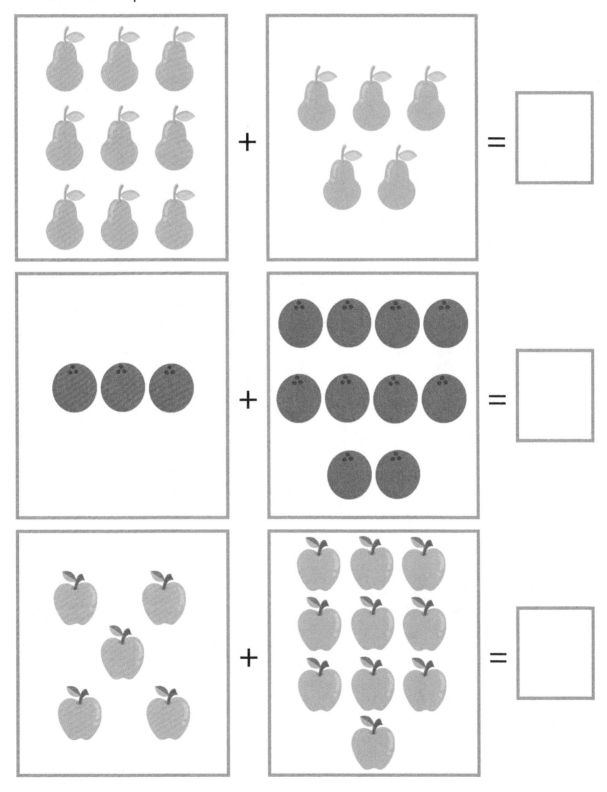

ADDITION TO 15

Count the pictures. Add and write the correct sum in the box.

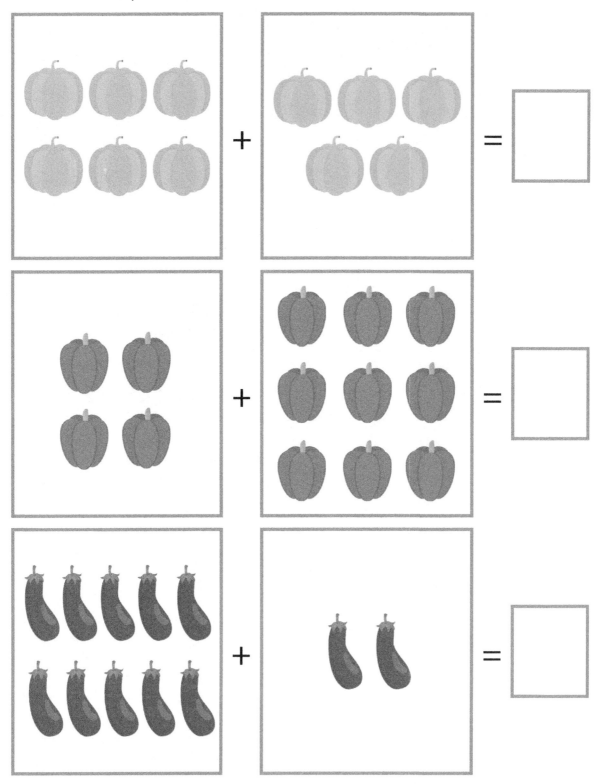

ADDITION TO 15

Count the pictures. Add and write the correct sum in the box.

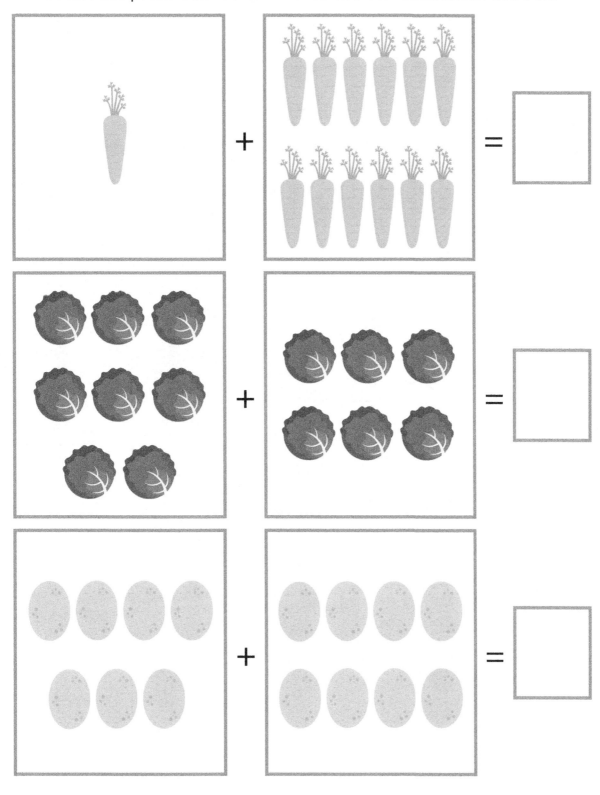

ADDITION TO 15

Count the pictures. Add and write the correct sum in the box.

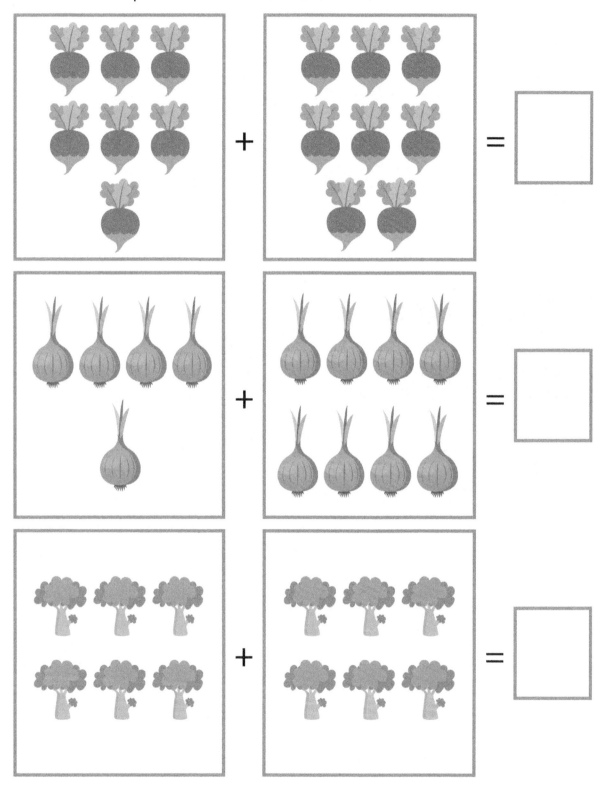

ADDITION TO 15

Count the pictures. Add and write the correct sum in the box.

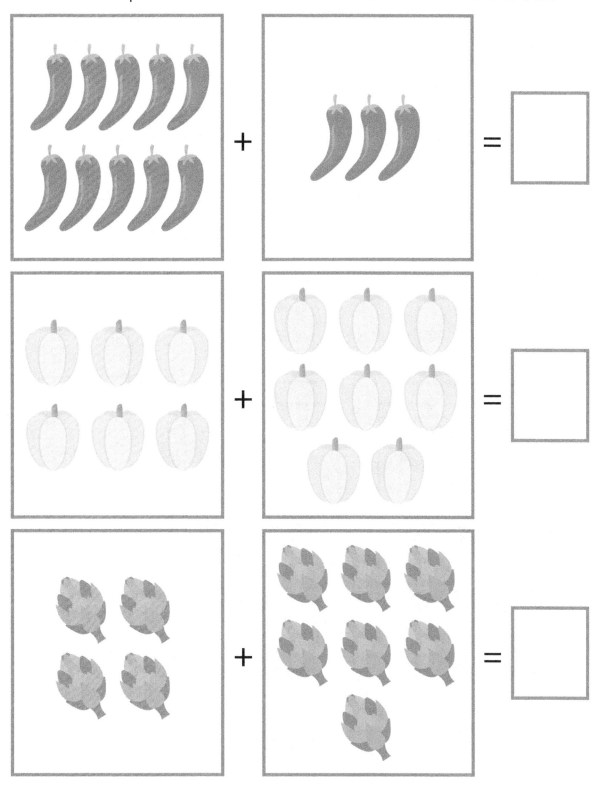

ADDITION TO 20

Count the pictures. Add and write the correct sum in the box.

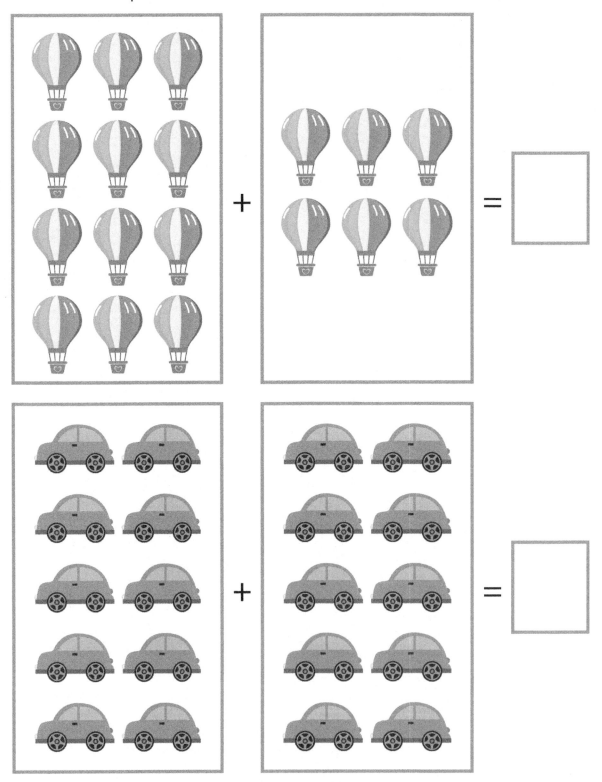

ADDITION TO 20

Count the pictures. Add and write the correct sum in the box.

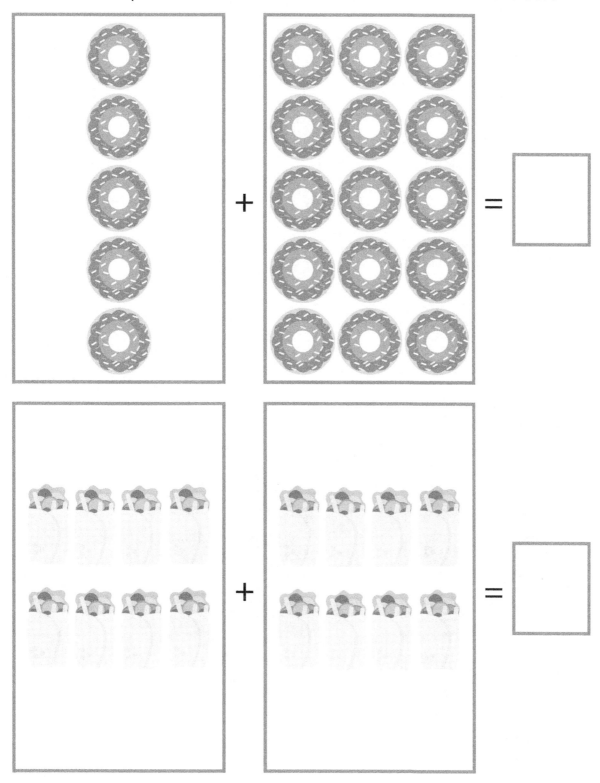

ADDITION TO 20

Count the pictures. Add and write the correct sum in the box.

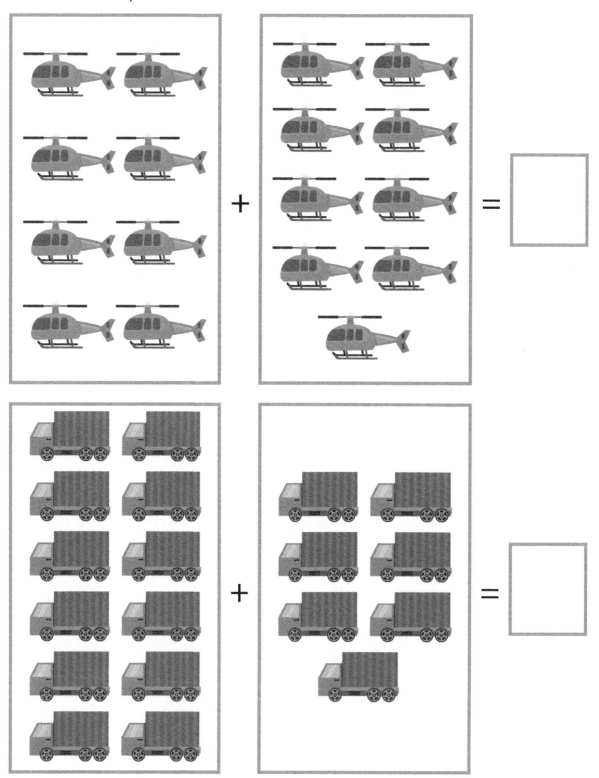

ADDITION TO 20

Count the pictures. Add and write the correct sum in the box.

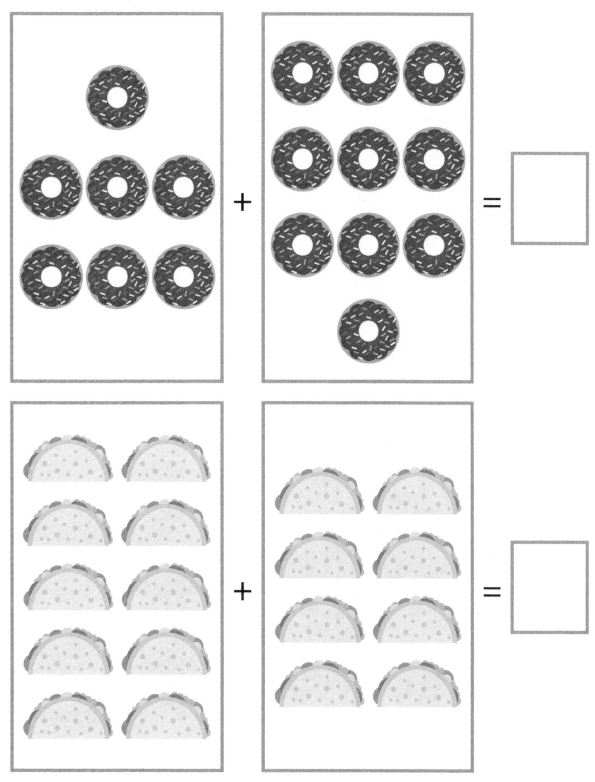

ADDITION TO 20

Count the pictures. Add and write the correct sum in the box.

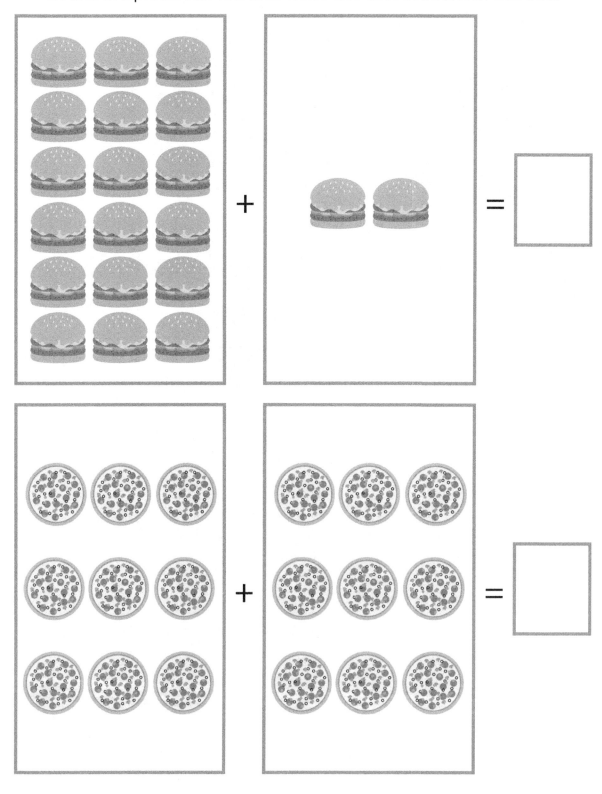

SUBTRACTION

Subtract and write the correct answer in the box.

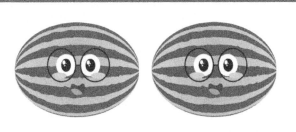 2-1 =

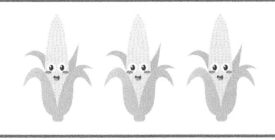 3-1 =

 4-3 =

 5-1 =

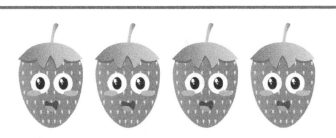 4-2 =

SUBTRACTION

Subtract and write the correct answer in the box.

 4-1 =

 3-3 =

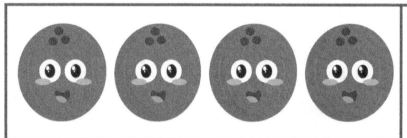 4-2 =

 4-3 =

 5-3 =

SUBTRACTION

Subtract and write the correct answer in the box.

 | 3-2 =

 | 5-2 =

 | 5-3 =

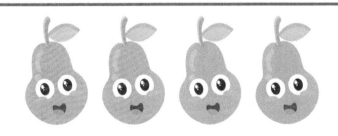 | 4-4 =

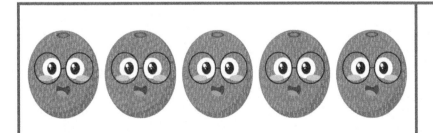 | 5-5 =

SUBTRACTION

Subtract and write the correct answer in the box.

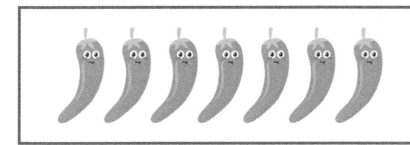 7-2 =

 9-4 =

 8-3 =

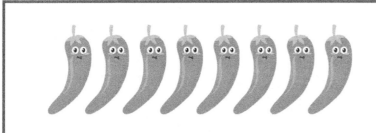 8-5 =

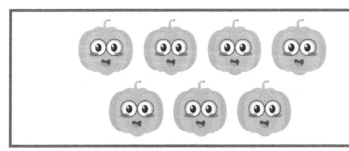 7-3 =

SUBTRACTION

Subtract and write the correct answer in the box.

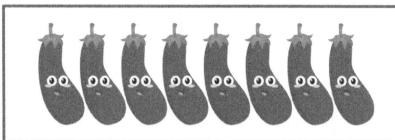 8-4 =

 9-5 =

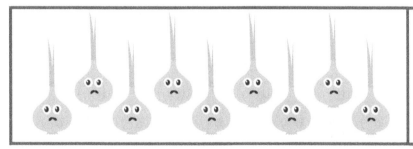 9-6 =

 7-5 =

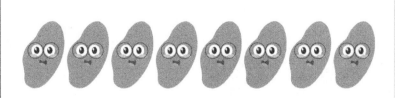 8-6 =

SUBTRACTION

Subtract and write the correct answer in the box.

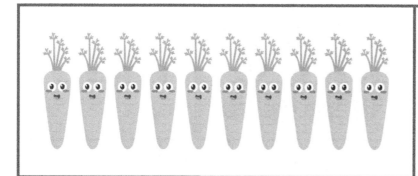 10-8 =

 9-7 =

 9-4 =

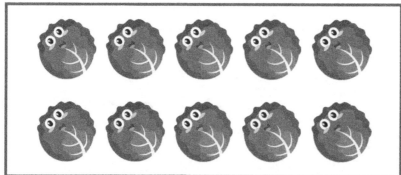 10-6 =

SUBTRACTION

Subtract and write the correct answer in the box.

 11-7 =

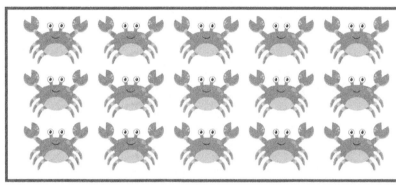 15-6 =

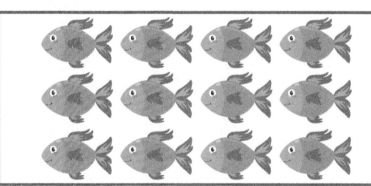 12-6 =

 11-5 =

SUBTRACTION

Subtract and write the correct answer in the box.

 10-3 =

 12-6 =

 14-2 =

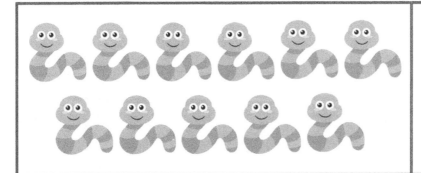 11-7 =

SUBTRACTION

Subtract and write the correct answer in the box.

 | 13-8 =

 | 14-7 =

 | 16-6 =

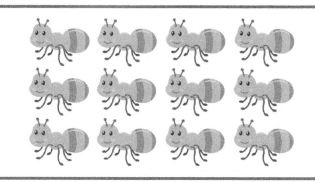 | 12-3 =

SUBTRACTION

Subtract and write the correct answer in the box.

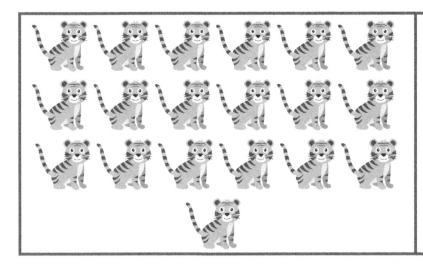

19-15 =

17-10 =

18-11 =

SUBTRACTION

Subtract and write the correct answer in the box.

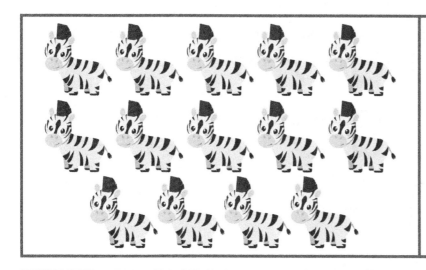 14-12 =

 13-13 =

 18-15 =

SUBTRACTION

Subtract and write the correct answer in the box.

 14-11 =

 13-10 =

 15-11 =

SUBTRACTION

Subtract and write the correct answer in the box.

 15-12 =

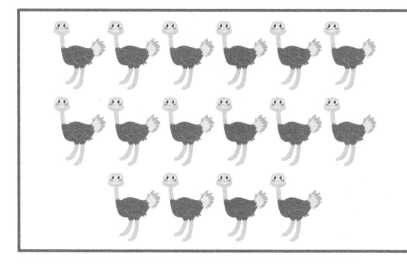 16-14 =

 18-10 =

SUBTRACTION

Subtract and write the correct answer in the box.

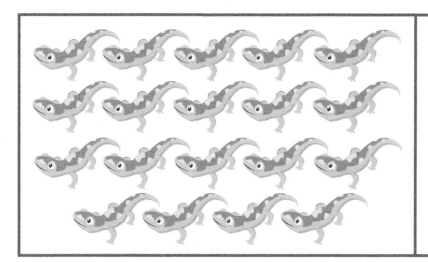 19-11 =

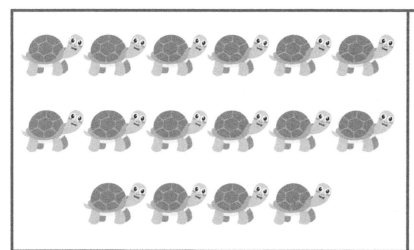 16-14 =

 17-10 =

SUBTRACTION

Subtract and write the correct answer in the box.

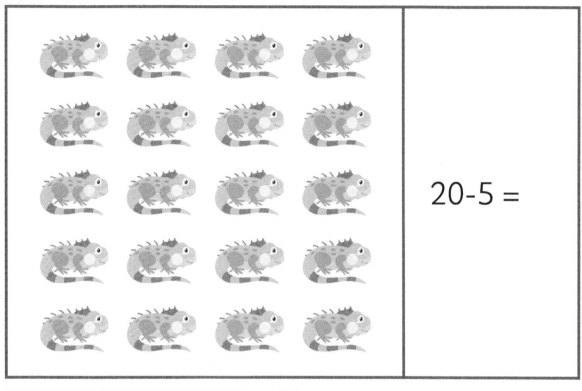

20-5 =

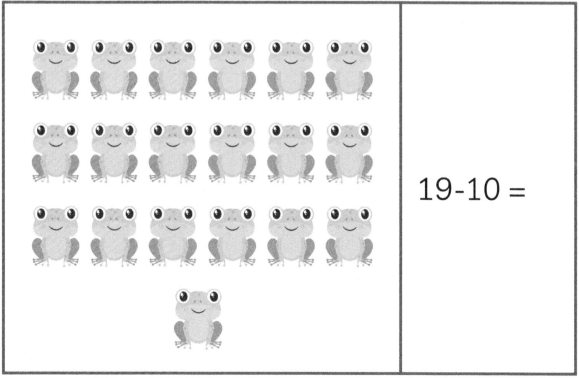

19-10 =

SUBTRACTION

Subtract and write the correct answer in the box.

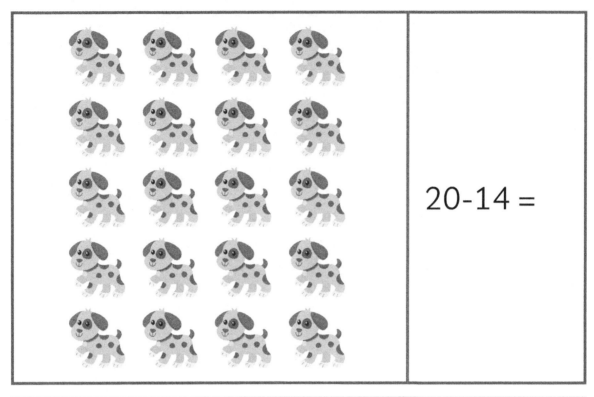

20-14 =

17-11 =

SUBTRACTION

Subtract and write the correct answer in the box.

17-4 =

16-9 =

SUBTRACTION

Subtract and write the correct answer in the box.

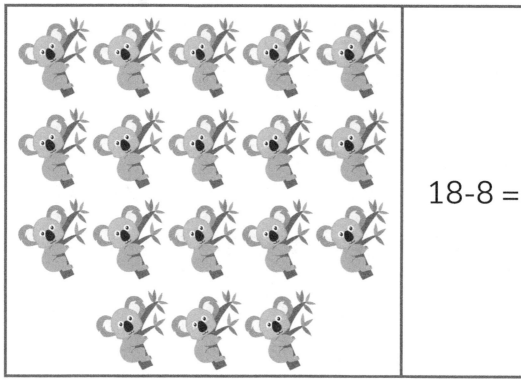

18-8 =

17-13 =

SUBTRACTION

Subtract and write the correct answer in the box.

20-5 =

19-10 =

AB PATTERNS

Look at the patterns below. Cut out the images at the bottom.
Paste the image that comes next in each pattern.

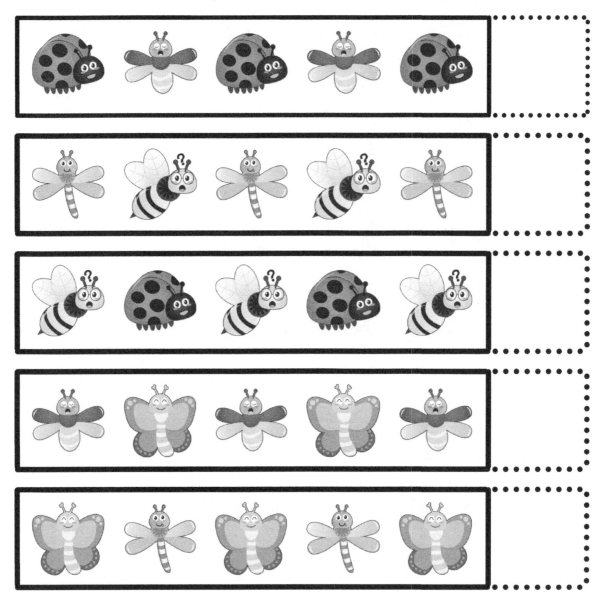

AB PATTERNS

Look at the patterns below. Cut out the images at the bottom.
Paste the image that comes next in each pattern.

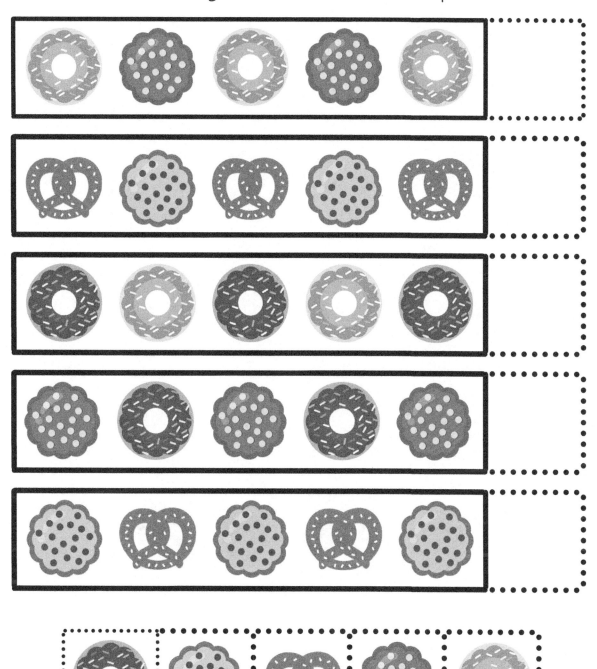

AAB PATTERNS

Look at the patterns below. Cut out the images at the bottom.
Paste the image that comes next in each pattern.

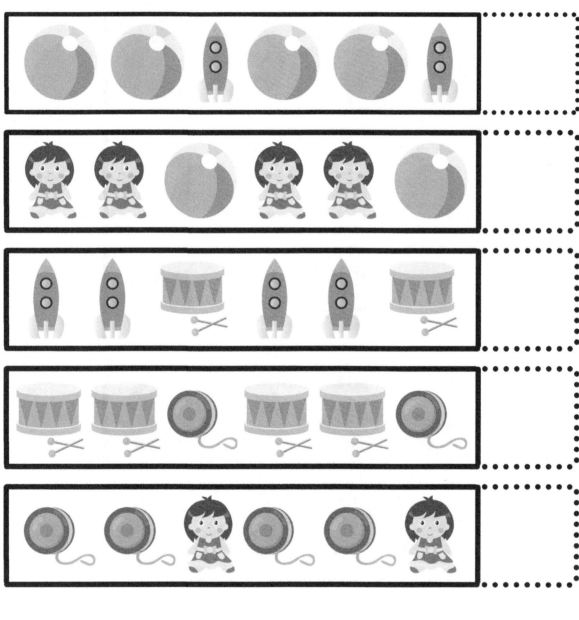

AAB PATTERNS

Look at the patterns below. Cut out the images at the bottom.
Paste the image that comes next in each pattern.

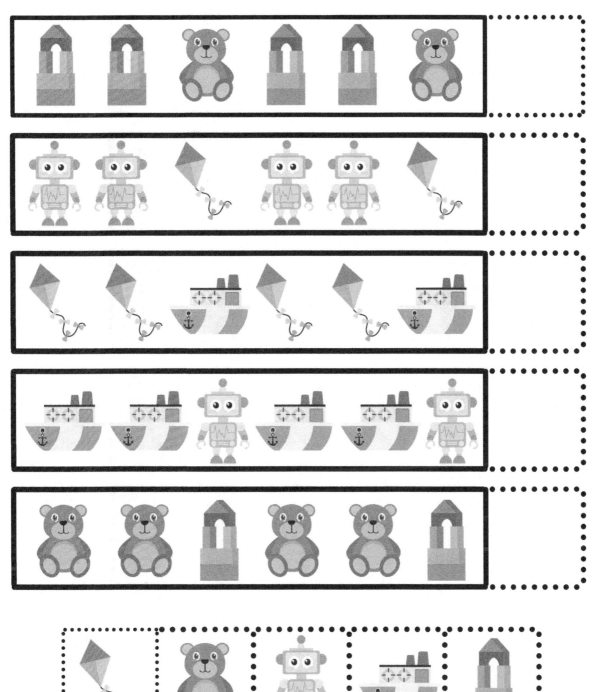

AAB PATTERNS

Look at the patterns below. Cut out the images at the bottom.
Paste the image that comes next in each pattern.

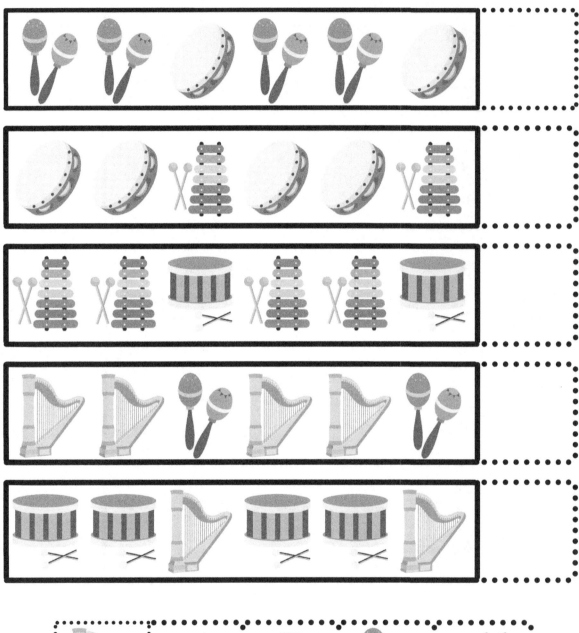

ABB PATTERNS

Look at the patterns below. Cut out the images at the bottom.
Paste the image that comes next in each pattern.

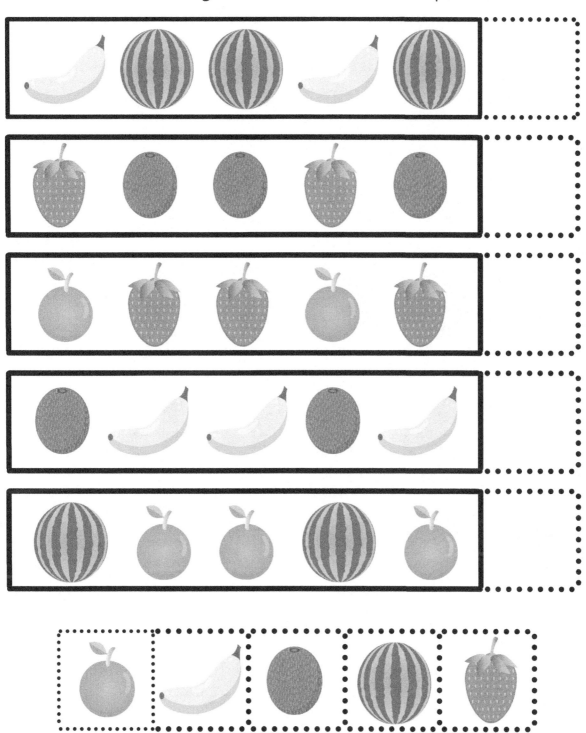

ABB PATTERNS

Look at the patterns below. Cut out the images at the bottom.
Paste the image that comes next in each pattern.

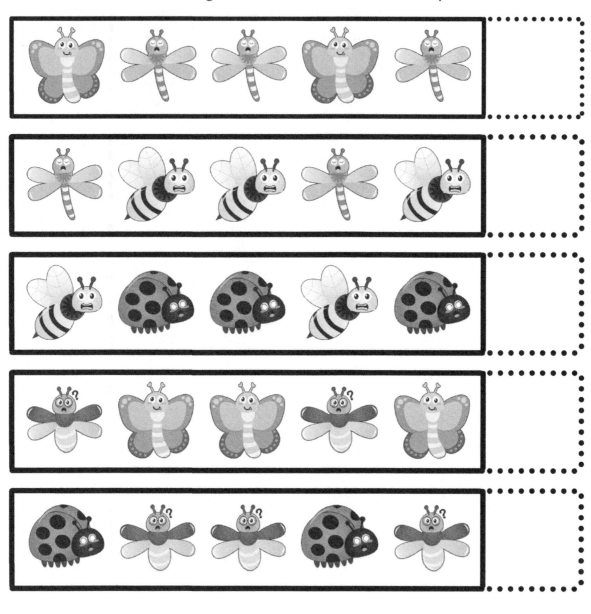

ABB PATTERNS

Look at the patterns below. Cut out the images at the bottom.
Paste the image that comes next in each pattern.

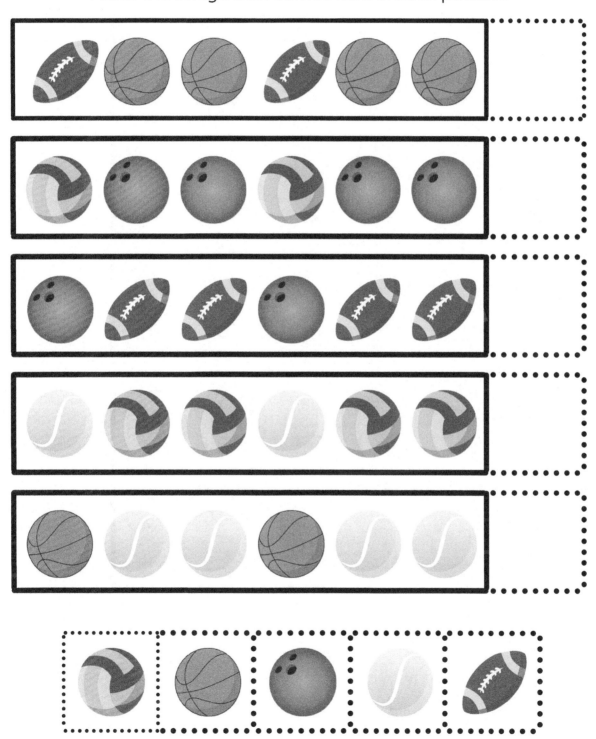

ABC PATTERNS

Look at the patterns below. Cut out the images at the bottom.
Paste the image that comes next in each pattern.

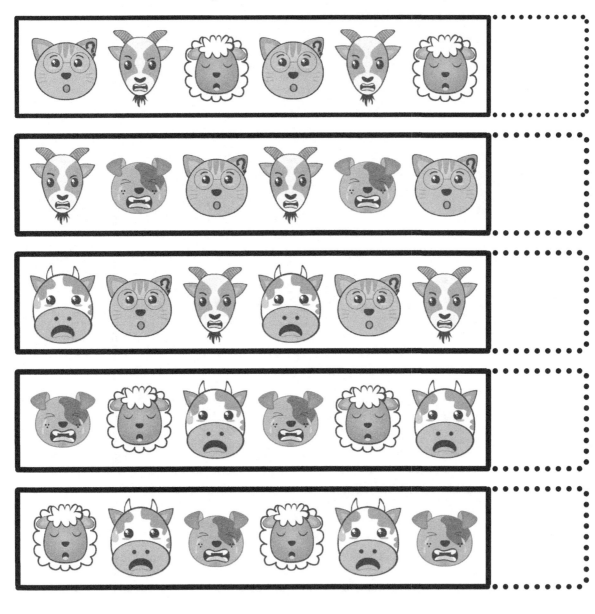

ABC PATTERNS

Look at the patterns below. Cut out the images at the bottom.
Paste the image that comes next in each pattern.

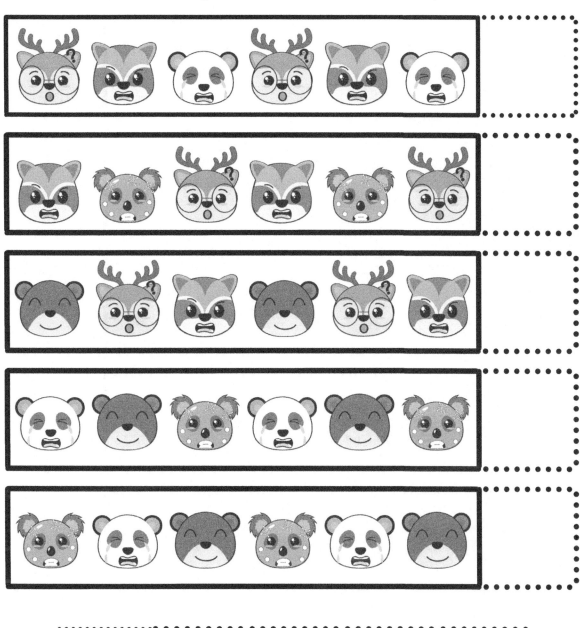

AABB PATTERNS

Look at the patterns below. Cut out the images at the bottom.
Paste the image that comes next in each pattern.

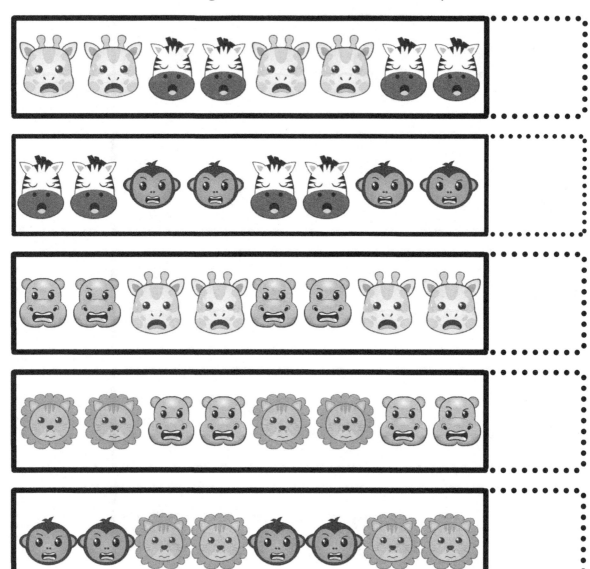

AABB PATTERNS

Look at the patterns below. Cut out the images at the bottom.
Paste the image that comes next in each pattern.

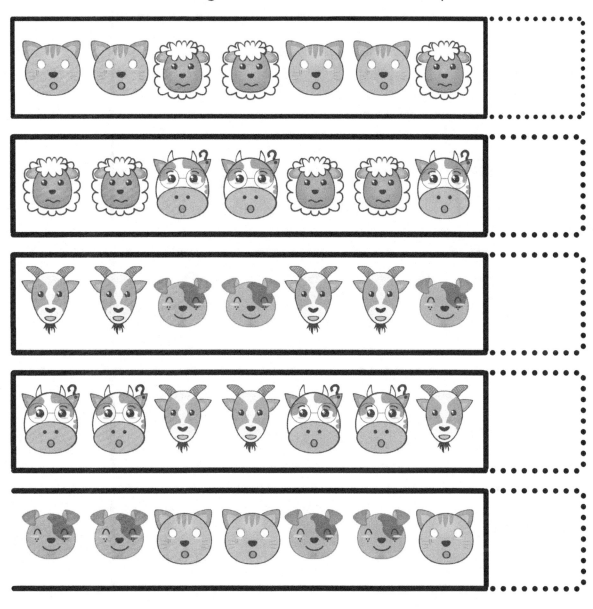

AABC PATTERNS

Look at the patterns below. Cut out the images at the bottom.
Paste the image that comes next in each pattern.

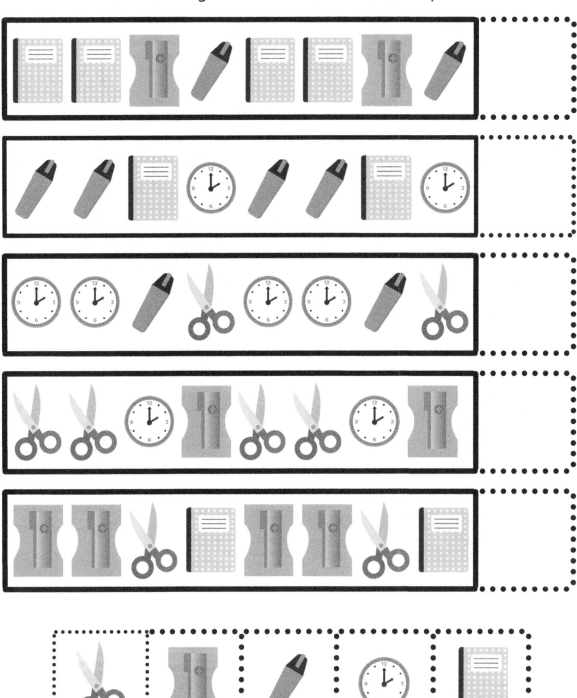

AABC PATTERNS

Look at the patterns below. Cut out the images at the bottom.
Paste the image that comes next in each pattern.

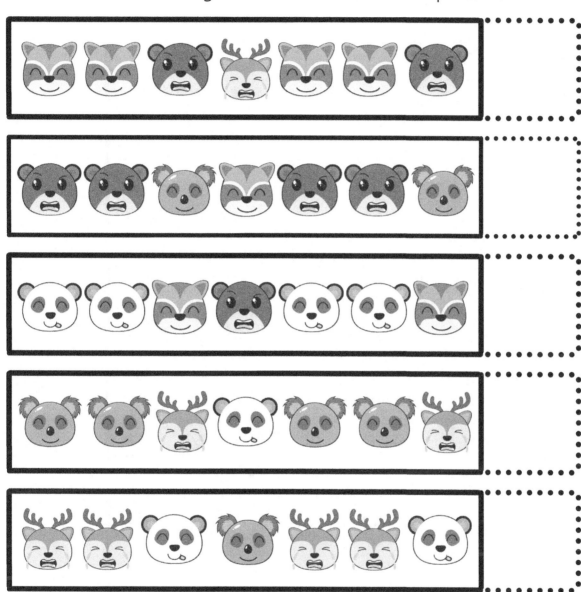

ABBC PATTERNS

Look at the patterns below. Cut out the images at the bottom.
Paste the image that comes next in each pattern.

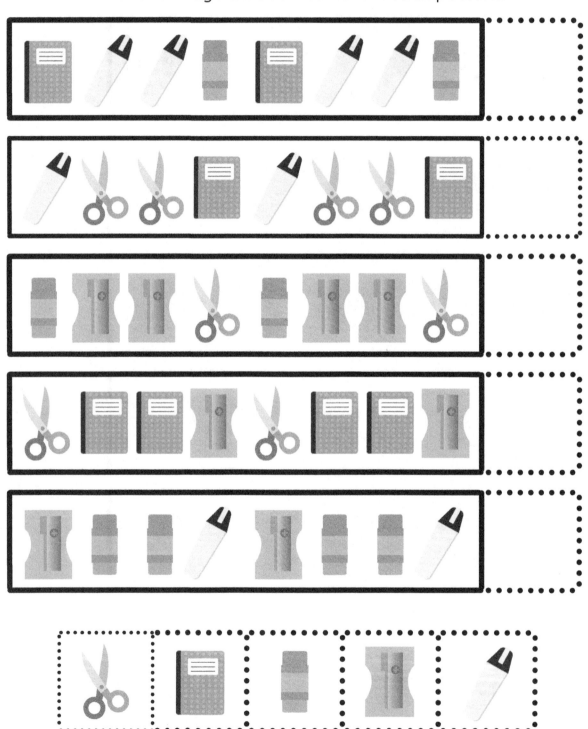

ABBC PATTERNS

Look at the patterns below. Cut out the images at the bottom.
Paste the image that comes next in each pattern.

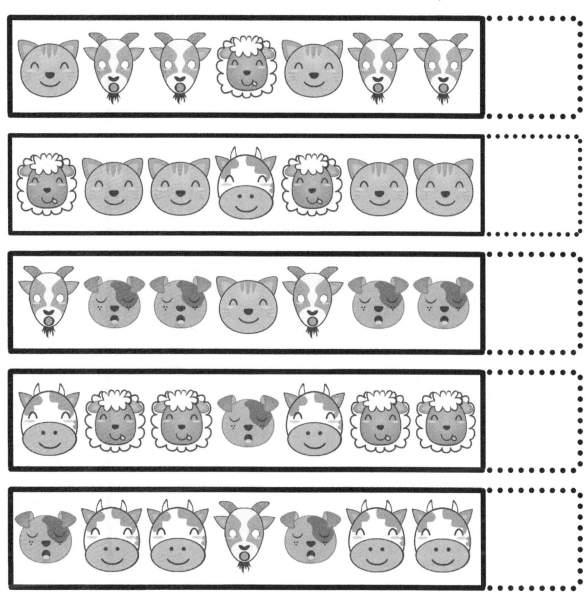

ABCD PATTERNS

Look at the patterns below. Cut out the images at the bottom.
Paste the image that comes next in each pattern.

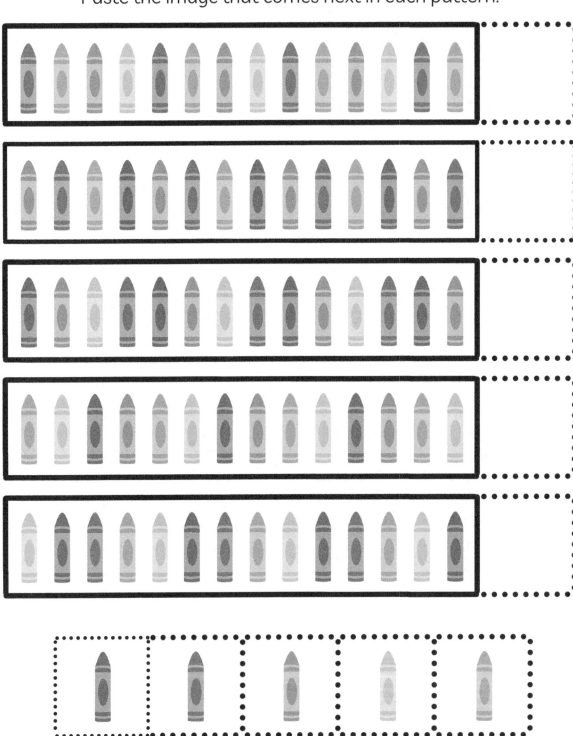

ABCD PATTERNS

Look at the patterns below. Cut out the images at the bottom.
Paste the image that comes next in each pattern.

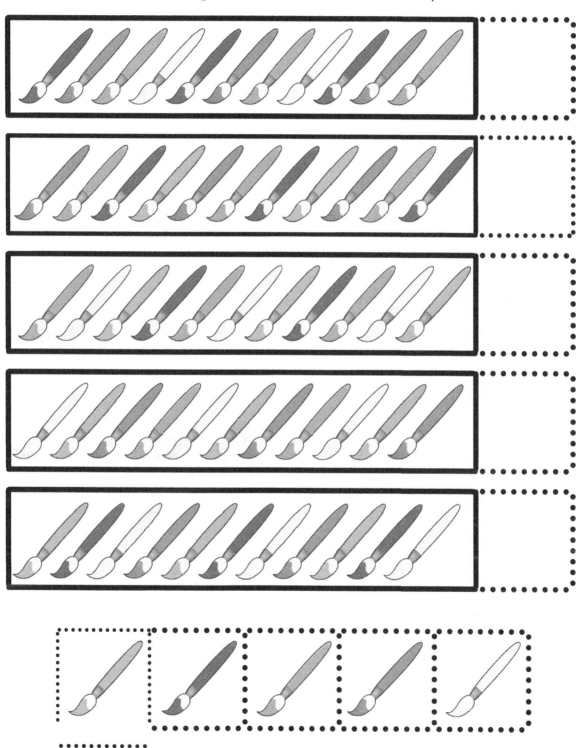

2D SHAPE TRACING

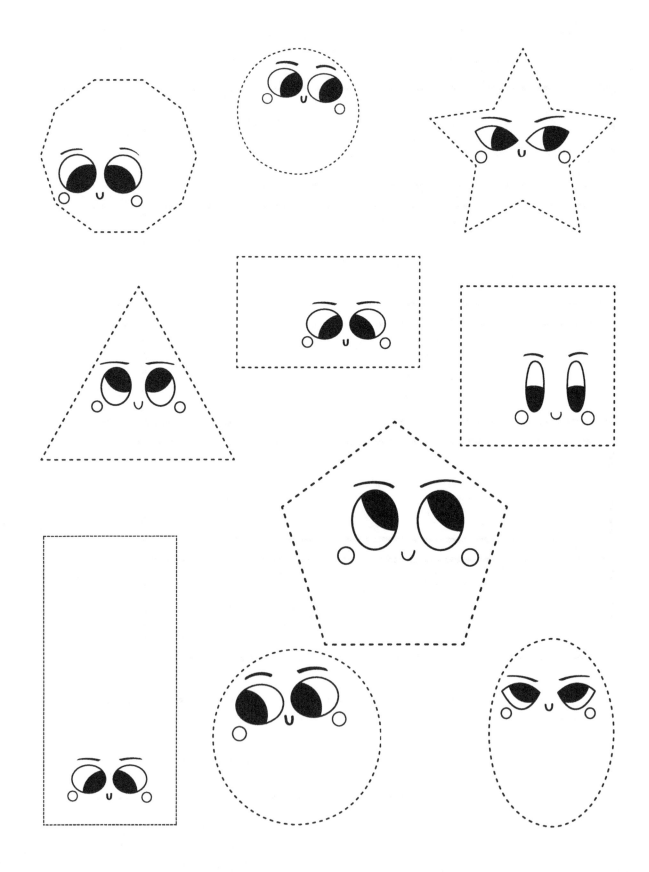

2D SHAPE NAMES

Trace   Trace   Write   Draw

circle

triangle

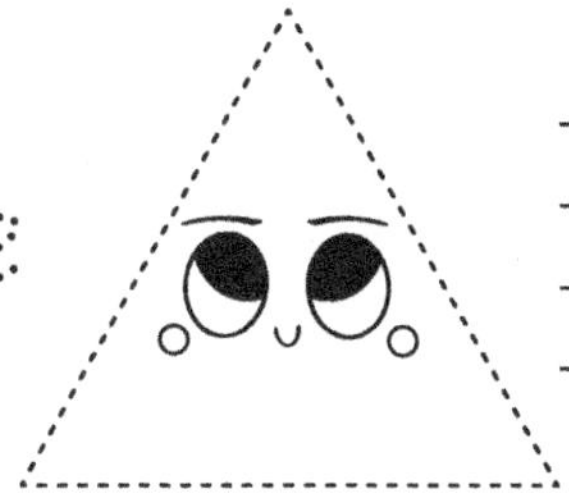

square

rectangle

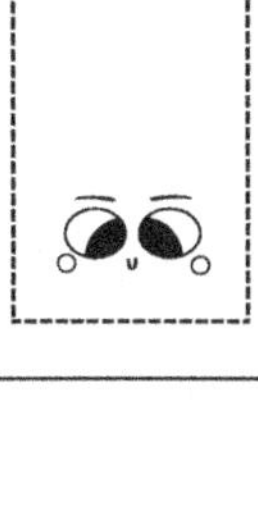

2D SHAPE RECOGNITION

Instructions: How many of the following shapes do you see in each image below?

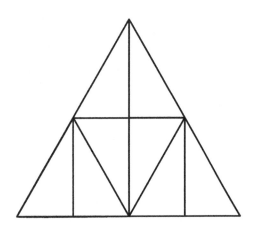

Triangles:

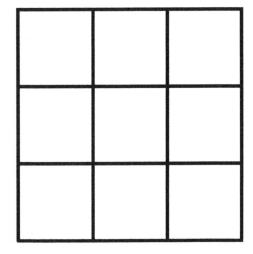

Squares:

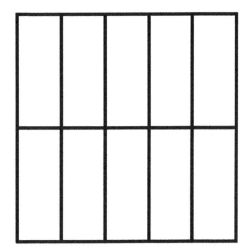

Rectangles:

2D SHAPE RECOGNITION

Instructions: Colour the shapes the following colours:

Circles: Yellow   Rectangles: Green   Triangles: Blue   Squares: Pink

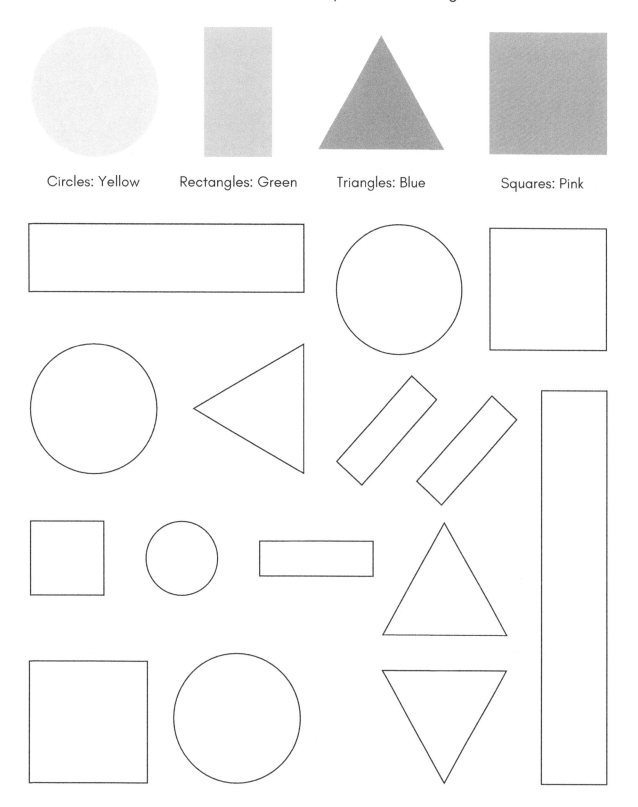

2D SHAPE RECOGNITION

Instructions: How many of the following shapes do you see in the picture below?

Triangles: Squares: Rectangles   Circles:

2D SHAPE RECOGNITION

Instructions: Circle all the triangles below:

Sphere

sphere

sphere

sphere

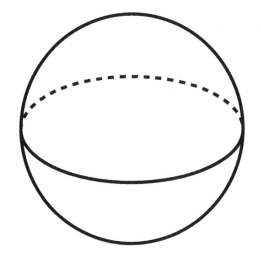

Vertices	
Curved Surfaces	
Edges	

Colour the spheres.

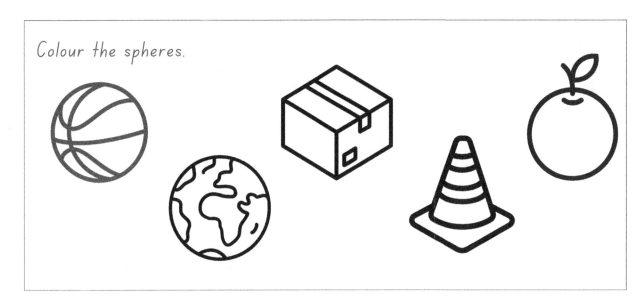

Draw some real-world spheres below:

3D SHAPE RECOGNITION

Cube

cube

cube

cube

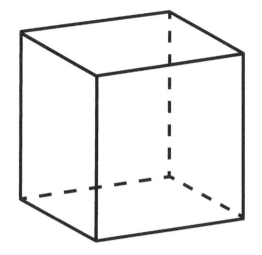

Vertices	
Faces	
Edges	

Colour the cubes:

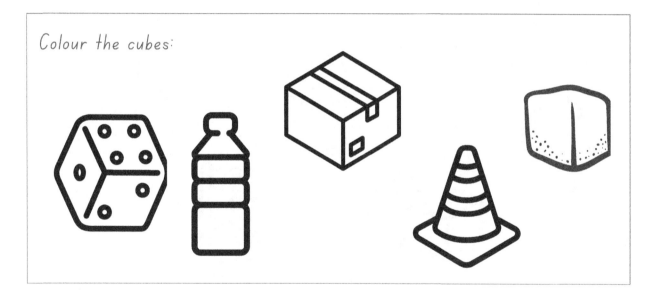

Draw some real-world cubes below:

3D SHAPE RECOGNITION

Rectangular Prism

prism

prism

prism

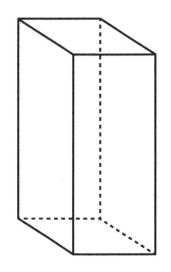

Vertices	
Faces	
Edges	

Colour the rectangular prisms:

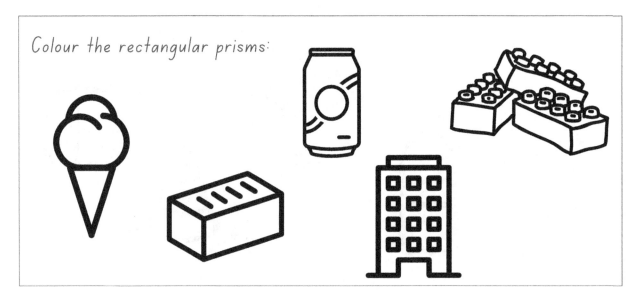

Draw some real-world prisms below:

3D SHAPE RECOGNITION

Cone

cone

cone

cone

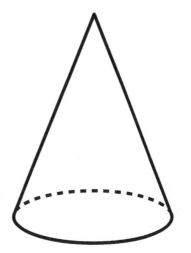

Apex	
Curved Surfaces	
Edges	

Colour the cones:

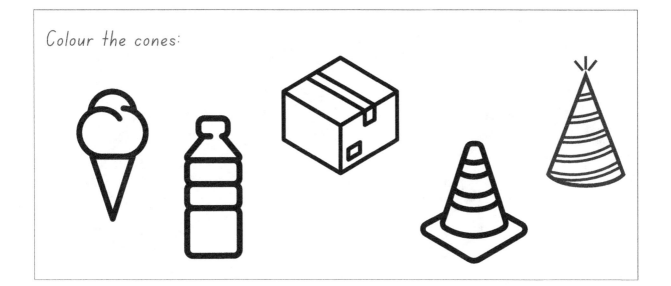

Draw some real-world cones below:

3D SHAPE RECOGNITION

Square-Based Pyramid

pyramid

pyramid

pyramid

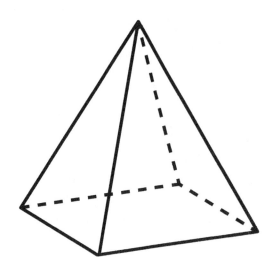

Vertices	
Faces	
Edges	

Colour the pyramids:

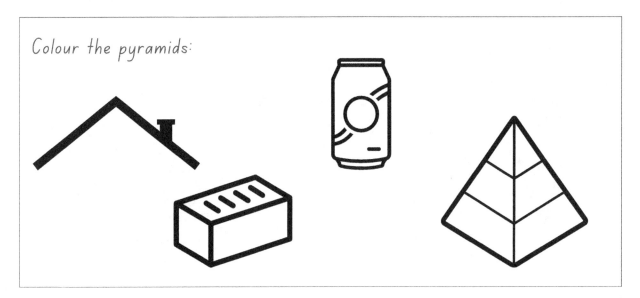

Draw some real-world pyramids below:

3D SHAPE RECOGNITION

Cylinder

cylinder

cylinder

cylinder

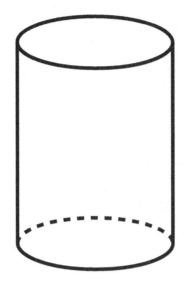

Vertices	
Curved Surfaces	
Faces	

Colour the cylinders.

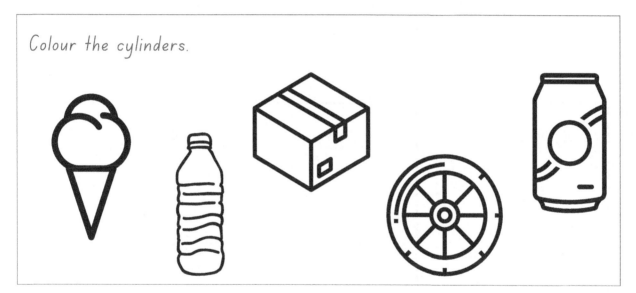

Draw some real-world cylinders below:

3D SHAPE RECOGNITION

3D SHAPE RECOGNITION

3D SHAPES

Write the amount of faces, edges and vertices for each 3d shape.

CYLINDER

Eaces _____
Edges _____
Vertices _____

CONE

_____
_____
_____

CUBE

Faces _____
Edges _____
Vertices _____

SPHERE

Faces _____
Edges _____
Vertices _____

CUBOID

Faces _____
Edges _____
Vertices _____

PYRAMID

Faces _____
Edges _____
Vertices _____

TRIANGULAR PRISM

Faces _____
Edges _____
Vertices _____

PENTAGONAL PRISM

Faces _____
Edges _____
Vertices _____

HEXAGONAL PRISM

Faces _____
Edges _____
Vertices _____

3D SHAPE RECOGNITION

3D SHAPES

Match each 3D shape with its name.

CYLINDER

SPHERE

PENTAGONAL PRISM

CUBOID

PYRAMID

TRIANGULAR PRISM

HEXAGONAL PRISM

CONE

CUBE

Made in United States
North Haven, CT
06 June 2025

69565123R00122